# MELBOURNE SCHOOL OF THEOLOGY

*PARADOSIS*

**Volume No. 1**

**2014**

**PARADOSIS**

No 1. (2014)

ISSN 2203-4951
ISBN 978-0-9924763-0-4
© 2014 Melbourne School of Theology. All rights reserved.

**Executive Editor**
Justin Tan

**Principal Editor**
Colin Kruse

**Issue Editor**
Greg Forbes

**Assistant Editor**
Liz Burley

**Production and Cover Design**
Ho-yuin Chan

**A Publication of the Melbourne School of Theology**
5 Burwood Highway, Wantirna, Victoria 3152, Australia.
PO Box 6257, Vermont Sth, Victoria 3133, Australia
Ph: +61 3 9881 7800, Fax: +61 3 9800 0121
mstpress@mst.edu.au, www.mst.edu.au

---

Opinions and conclusions published in PARADOSIS are those of the authors and do not necessarily represent the views of the Editors or the Melbourne School of Theology.

| | |
|---|---|
| Principal Editor's Introduction to *PARADOSIS* | 4 |
| Editorial | 6 |

Features

Dead Commentator's Society: Is There a Formal Place for Reception History in Evangelical Biblical Exegesis?
*Andrew Brown*.................................................... 8

Paul the Law and the Spirit
*Colin Kruse*...................................................... 28

The Theological Interpretation of Scripture with Special Attention to the Pioneering Insights of Athanasius and Augustine
*Kevin Giles*...................................................... 49

Adultery, Divorce, and the Hard-Hearted People of God: The Function of the Matthean Exemption Clause (Matt 19:9) in its Literary Context
*David W. Pao*.................................................... 64

The Knowledge of God in St. Basil's *De Spiritu Sancto*
*Murray Hogg*.................................................... 83

God as Husband and Jesus as Bridegroom: A Critical Reassessment of the Divine Conjugal Metaphor
*Gillian Asquith*.................................................. *105*

| | |
|---|---|
| Invitation for Papers | 131 |
| Notes for Contributors | 132 |

# PRINCIPAL EDITOR'S INTRODUCTION TO *PARADOSIS*

The Melbourne School of Theology (MST) is committed to pursuing excellence in learning, research and the highest possible standard of scholarship in theological education, an area in which we are called to make a contribution to the work of the Gospel.

MST is launching a new journal entitled *PARADOSIS*, a Greek word meaning 'tradition'. *PARADOSIS* is chosen as the title of the journal because it expresses the sense that the theological enterprise is a continuous ministry, the ongoing 'traditioning' responsibility of the Christian church to carry forward the deposit of faith from the past, while rearticulating it in dialogue with the contexts, mindsets and issues of current culture.

Admittedly, 'tradition' can have negative connotations, as in Jesus' criticisms of Scribes and Pharisees who broke the commandments of God for the sake of their human traditions. However, it has positive connotations when used in relation to the gospel of Christ and the fundamental Christian teachings received and passed on by the apostles. These form the bedrock of the Christian faith. Early believers were urged to hold fast to, contend for, and pass on this tradition.

The theological implications of the gospel traditions occupied the best minds in Christendom during the early centuries following the apostolic age. The consensual conclusions they reached constitute Christian orthodoxy and the basis of subsequent theological endeavours down through the Middle Ages, the Reformation period, the Enlightenment, and the theological enterprise today.

Christian theology must serve pastoral ministry, evangelism, cross cultural mission and inter-faith dialogue. From the earliest centuries Christian leaders, evangelists and apologists sought to apply theology to the pastoral needs of believers and commend the faith to others. In recent times these disciplines have flourished and are producing their own traditions.

*PARADOSIS* will showcase articles in Biblical studies and theology. A future journal planned by MST, *PRAXIS*, will provide opportunity for the publication of articles in pastoral ministry, evangelism, mission and other living faiths.

Dr Colin G. Kruse
Principal Editor

# Editorial

This inaugural issue of *PARADOSIS* contains several articles, all dealing in various ways with applied hermeneutics.

Andrew Brown laments the lack of attention given in modern day exegesis to the history of interpretation of a given text. Such a neglect of "reception history," he points out, is often the product of an evolutionary approach to biblical studies whereby the "newer' is virtually synonymous with the "better" and the "older" with the "inferior." But we are part of an interpretive community with a long and rich history, and we neglect the labours of those who have gone before us to our own detriment.

In a paper written from the perspective of one who has spent the major portion of his academic life devoted to the study of Paul and Pauline literature, Colin Kruse presents a helpful synthesis of Paul's teaching on the relationship of the Mosaic Law and the reception of the Spirit. In so doing he employs the reformation ideal of scriptural interpretation whereby "scripture interprets scripture." Kruse insists that passages in Romans, Galatians and 2 Corinthians are mutually illuminating and together supply a view of the Law and the Spirit that are at the same time both complex yet consistent.

The essay by Kevin Giles is a veteran's reflection upon his voyage of discovery regarding the place of the Bible in theological interpretation. Or, to put the matter differently, he provides an assessment of what a "theological interpretation of Scripture" entails. Giles does not so much engage in an interaction with current scholarship on the issue, but examines the processes employed by two of the outstanding post-Nicene fathers, Athanasius and Augustine. Giles concludes that the theological interpretation of Scripture involves an approach to the Bible that takes proper account of its unity in diversity, duly recognises the history of interpretation, and is aware of both the role and limitations of analogy and metaphor.

In a thought-provoking study on the Matthean exemption clause (Matt 19:1-12), David Pao contends that the passage should be understood against a covenantal framework of fidelity and apostasy. Taking its cue from the surrounding literary context, together with echoes of several OT prophetic traditions, the exemption clause functions as a call for the unfaithful of Israel to repent, particularly with respect to their non-acceptance of Jesus as Messiah.

Murray Hogg examines Basil of Caesarea's (ca. 329-379CE) *De Spiritu Sancto* (374CE) in order to ascertain Basil's understanding of epistemology or, more narrowly, his understanding of what is involved in the Christian's knowledge of God. He suggests that Basil's epistemology is non-reductionist, holistic, and coherentist in nature. The study concludes with some consideration of the important consequences which follow from its findings.

Gillian Asquith presents an informative analysis of the divine conjugal metaphor in both the Old and New Testaments. She shows how the OT employment of the metaphor is used predominately in the context of Israel's covenant infidelity and God's covenant faithfulness and grace. This provides the background for the NT usage of the metaphor, where Christ is presented as bridegroom or husband of the church.

Dr Greg Forbes
Issue Editor

# Features

## Dead Commentators' Society: Is There a Formal Place for Reception History in Evangelical Biblical Exegesis?

Andrew Brown

Melbourne School of Theology

Abstract:

*One literary theory that has affected mainstream biblical studies in recent decades is what is often called 'Reception History'. But it has only achieved very limited penetration in evangelical texts that outline the process of Old Testament exegesis for theological students. The exegetical methodology of theological students is arguably the poorer for this omission. Reception history is a methodology of sufficient merit to warrant deliberate incorporation into the exegetical process that is taught to students, being both informed by contemporary philosophy and aligning well with long-standing traditional Christian interpretive practice. It encourages an attitude of humility and teachability that augments the present reader's understanding of the biblical text with the oft-neglected wisdom of earlier commentators, and takes practical note of the historical interface of the Bible with wider culture.*

**Synopsis**

One of the more recent developments out of literary theory to impact biblical studies is what is usually called 'Reception History'. It has made its mark sporadically since the 1970s in the English-speaking domain, but has only achieved very limited penetration in evangelical texts that outline the process of biblical, and particularly Old Testament, exegesis for theological students. The exegetical methodology of theological students is arguably the poorer for this omission. Reception history is a methodology that is promising enough to warrant deliberate incorporation into the exegetical process that is taught to students, being both informed by contemporary philosophy and well supported by long-standing traditional practice within the Christian Church. It encourages an attitude of humility and teachability that does not assume that either the present generation of Christian readers or the individual reader alone is fully equipped to explain the meaning of the biblical text, to the neglect of the widely-acknowledged wisdom of earlier commentators.

**Introduction**

"If a tree falls in the forest, and there is no-one to hear it, does it make a sound?" Thus Lisa Simpson challenged her brother Bart with the famous existential conundrum, to which Bart replied, 'Sure', and duplicated the sound.[1] While he went on to be enlightened by the New Age Lisa, the critical realist still wants to defend the real-world reality of the shattering noise, with or without an audience.

It is not quite so simple with texts. Where a text is seen as an act of communication, and I would argue that most written texts are, it has not really succeeded at communicating until someone has heard or read the text and apprehended its meaning in some way.[2] Until then it is simply a potential communicative act. The words are on the paper, but it has not made a communicative sound until it reaches an audience with an effect commensurate with its purpose.

The role of the audience or reader of a text has been a central interest of contemporary philosophy and a particular emphasis of postmodern thought, sometimes to the neglect of other factors such as the career of the text itself, author intention, or in the case of Scripture, divine superintendence. Such is often the case with pendulum-like corrections. But when restrained from a headlong plunge into utter subjectivity, the field of literary theory (or hermeneutics, the study of interpretation) called 'reader response theory' can offer a helpful corrective to a simplistic view of the way authors communicate via texts.

'Reception history' is often classed as one of several reader-response approaches.[3] There is some warrant for this; one of the

---

[1] See http://www.whyfaith.com/2006/08/30/if-a-tree-falls-in-a-forest-riddle-answered/ and the footnote there.

[2] This is the governing idea in the hermeneutics text, Jeannine K. Brown, *Scripture as Communication: Introducing Biblical Hermeneutics* (Grand Rapids: Baker Academic, 2007).

[3] E.g. J. Barton, *Reading the Old Testament: Method in Biblical Study*, Revised and enlarged ed. (Louisville: Westminster John Knox, 1996), 212-214; Anthony Thiselton, *Hermeneutics: An Introduction* (Grand Rapids: Eerdmans, 2009), 306-326. By contrast, it appears in a different section to the reader-oriented methods in David A. Holgate and Rachel Starr, *SCM Studyguide to Biblical Hermeneutics* (London: SCM, 2006), 83-88.

philosophers whose work lies at the foundation of the field of reception history is Hans-Georg Gadamer (1900-2002), whose *Truth and Method* (German original 1960) had its own impressive reception amongst hermeneutical theorists both sacred and secular, not least the above-cited Anthony Thiselton. Gadamer offered a controlled exploration of the role of the reader in constituting textual meaning, and he was the populariser of the German term *Wirkungsgeschichte* or 'impact history' that has become one of the key terms of reception history.[4] His student Hans Robert Jauss (1921-1997), one of a circle of literary theorists based in the University of Konstanz in Germany, became the patron figure of reception history, and his writings constitute the theoretical texts that undergird this interpretive approach.[5]

The way 'reception history' is presently understood and employed becomes clearer when we compare it to an older tradition of studying the history of biblical interpretation typified by works such as Frederick W. Farrar's *History of Interpretation* (1886).[6] A good, early example from my own field of study, the interpretation of the creation week (Gen. 1:1-2:3) is F. Robbins, *The Hexaemeral Literature* (1915).[7] The early 1900s saw one or two German theologians calling for the extension of such interpretive histories into the study of the impact of the Bible on the Christian Church, and not only of the Church's understanding of the Bible.[8] Then Gerhard Ebeling, in a 1947 lecture, asserted that church history in fact consisted of "the history of the exposition of holy Scripture."[9] Church historian Karlfried Froehlich sees this lecture as the prompt (though

---

[4] Hans-Georg Gadamer, *Truth and Method* (trans. Garrett Barden and John Cumming; London: Sheed & Ward, 1975), 267-274, 430.

[5] For book-length works in English translation, see Hans Robert Jauss, *Toward an Aesthetics of Reception*, (ed. Wlad Godzich and Jochen Schulte-Sasse; trans. Timothy Bahti; Theory and History of Literature, vol. 2; Minneapolis: University of Minnesota Press, 1982); Idem, *Aesthetic Experience and Literary Hermeneutics* (trans. Michael Shaw; Theory and History of Literature, vol. 3; Minneapolis: University of Minnesota Press, 1982); Idem, *Question and Answer: Forms of Dialogic Understanding* (Minneapolis: University of Minnesota Press, 1989).

[6] F. W. Farrar, *History of Interpretation* (London: Macmillan, 1886).

[7] F. Robbins, *The Hexaemeral Literature: A Study of the Greek and Latin Commentaries in Genesis* (Chicago: University of Chicago Press, 1912; repr., 1988).

[8] David P. Parris, *Reception Theory and Biblical Hermeneutics* (Eugene, OR: Pickwick Publications, 2009), ix-x.

[9] Karlfried Froehlich, "Church History and the Bible," in *Biblical Hermeneutics in Historical Perspective: Studies in Honor of Karlfried Froehlich on His Sixtieth Birthday* (ed. Mark S. Burrows and Paul Rorem; Grand Rapids: Eerdmans, 1991), 7-8.

unacknowledged) for a proposed methodology for 'history-of-interpretation' (*Auslegungsgeschichte*) offered by David Lerch and Lukas Vischer in 1955, and for more than one book series in Germany devoted to this theme, well before 'reception history' came to prominence.[10]

The meaning of the term 'reception history' in contemporary usage has shifted beyond this 'history of interpretation' approach in several ways. First, it asks not only how the social and personal contexts of interpreters have affected how they approach texts, but also how texts have impacted their readers, both individually and as communities and cultures, hence the associated term 'impact history', 'history of influence' or 'effective history/history of effect(s)' (all suggested translations of *Wirkungsgeschichte*).[11] It also seeks to broaden the search for the evidence of impact beyond the examples of written texts, for instance in genres such as biblical commentary, to a text's "history, reception and actualization in other media, 'in sermons, in canon law, in psalms, in art, in the actions and sufferings of the church'."[12] A third broadening of this field of study that is being called for now is to ask about the impact of texts other than biblical texts,[13] although the fact is that literary theorists such as Jauss and Gadamer were never thinking solely of biblical texts, as enthusiastically as their thought has been embraced by some biblical scholars.[14]

The kind of reception history that I would like to see incorporated deliberately into the process of biblical exegesis that we teach to theological students naturally concerns the 'reception' of biblical

---

[10] Notably Beiträge zur Geschichte der biblischen Exegese and Beiträge zur Geschichte der biblischen Hermeneutik, both published by Mohr Siebeck. Ibid., 8; David Lerch and Lukas Vischer, "Die Auslegungsgeschichte als notwendige theologische Aufgabe," *Studia Patristica* 1 (1957), 414-419.

[11] 'Impact history' is the term used by Holgate and Starr, *Studyguide*, 83. 'History of influence' and 'History of effect' appear as alternatives in Mark Knight, "*Wirkungsgeschichte*, Reception History, Reception Theory," *Journal for the Study of the New Testament* 33, no. 2 (2010), 138. Gadamer's English translators use 'effective history': Gadamer, *Truth and Method*, 267, 305, 414, etc.

[12] Internal quotation is from Ulrich Luz's seminal reception-historical commentary on Matthew. Heikki Räisänen, "The Effective 'History' of the Bible: A Challenge to Biblical Scholarship?," *Scottish Journal of Theology* 45 (1992), 310-311, with quote on latter page.

[13] Eric Rephhun et al., "Beyond Christianity, the Bible, and the Text: Urgent Tasks and New Orientations for Reception History," *Relegere: Studies in Religion and Reception* 1, no. 1 (2011).

[14] For further information on defining terms such as 'reception history' and 'reception theory', see Knight, "*Wirkungsgeschichte*," 137-139; Hans-Josef Klauck et al., eds., *The Encyclopedia of the Bible and Its Reception* (Berlin: De Gruyter, 2009-), ix-xi.

texts, and will need to continue to pay special attention to written texts whose purpose is biblical interpretation, such as commentaries, as well as reserving its greatest energy for thinking about our interpretive approach to the biblical text, before also considering the social and intellectual impact of the text. Does such a modest proposal warrant the label 'reception history' at all, or is it merely a contemporary application of 'history of interpretation'?[15] Where our approach ought to be broader than mere history of interpretation (*Auslegungsgeschichte*) is in its awareness and critical adoption of 'reception theory', the philosophical hermeneutics of figures such as Gadamer and Jauss and their interpreters within the field of biblical studies, such as Thiselton and now David Parris.[16] Their careful thinking-through of the role of the reader and of the way (biblical) interpretation works in the context of social communities can enhance the way we appropriate the heritage of past biblical interpreters.

### The Penetration of Reception History in Biblical Studies

Reception theory has made a rather slow and fitful penetration of the sphere of biblical studies, often eclipsed by other approaches, especially where perceived as merely a subset of reader-response theory or the hobby horse of one particular continental literary theorist (Jauss). In the wake of the publication in English translation of Jauss's key works, reception theory has found occasional advocates among biblical scholars,[17] and theoretical discussions have been mostly limited to New Testament thinkers such as Marcus Bockmuehl.[18] For instance, a 2010 issue of *Journal for the Study of the New Testament* was devoted to the issue. Even

---

[15] For advocacy of this kind of approach in biblical studies, see for example Michael Cahill, "The History of Exegesis and Our Theological Future," *Theological Studies* 61, no. 2 (2000), 332-347.

[16] Parris, *Reception Theory*. For a more popular handling, see David P. Parris, *Reading the Bible with Giants* (London: Paternoster, 2006).

[17] See for example Nigel M. Watson, "Reception Theory and Biblical Exegesis," *Australian Biblical Review* 36 (1988), 45-56.

[18] M. Bockmuehl, "'To Be or Not To Be': The Possible Futures of New Testament Scholarship," *Scottish Journal of Theology* 51 (1998), 295-296., where reception history appears to Bockmuehl to offer some promise to a field (New Testament studies) that he perceives to be involved in crisis. His thoughts are expressed in somewhat updated form in M. Bockmuehl, *Seeing the Word: Refocusing New Testament Study* (Grand Rapids: Baker Academic, 2006), 64-68.

texts devoted to biblical hermeneutics often make scant mention of reception theory or reception history up to the present day.[19]

However, as Mark Knight observes, reception theory and the undertaking of reception history can in practice be two separate things.[20] In contrast to the relative dearth of theoretical treatments of the implications of reception history for biblical studies, Parris' monograph offering one exception, there is a rapidly expanding assemblage of works that actually do reception-historical study of biblical texts. I have already mentioned that 'history-of-interpretation' works were proliferating in German series from the 1950s. In the English-speaking world, despite Froehlich's rather disparaging assessment, I see Brevard Childs' deliberate incorporation of the history of exegesis in dedicated sections, passage by passage, in his 1974 Exodus commentary as a noteworthy attempt to reintroduce what Froehlich calls "the text's post-history" into the process of biblical commentary.[21] Now we have the Ancient Christian Commentary on Scripture series offering sample patristic exegesis, the corresponding Reformation Commentary on Scripture, and the Blackwell Bible Commentaries offering a broad-brush reception history that includes art history and mainstream literature within its scope, as well as numerous individual reception-historical studies in monographs and journal articles, the *Oxford Handbook of the Reception History of the Bible* (2006) and the slowly-appearing *The Encyclopedia of the Bible and Its Reception* (2009-).

---

[19] For examples of limited and isolated treatments in recent works, see Susan Gillingham, *One Bible, Many Voices: Different Approaches to Biblical Studies* (London: SPCK, 1998), 183-184, although she herself practices reception history extensively even within the same work; Brown, *Scripture as Communication*, 65-74, but without any mention of reception history per se; Stanley E. Porter and Jason Robinson, *Hermeneutics: An Introduction to Interpretive Theory* (Grand Rapids: Eerdmans, 2011), 88-89. Works such as the last-mentioned and the following treat reader-response approaches in connection with another Konstanz figure, Wolfgang Iser, with limited or no specific reference to Jauss or reception history: Edgar V. McKnight, "Reader-Response Criticism," in *To Each Its Own Meaning: An Introduction to Biblical Criticisms and Their Applications* (ed. Stephen R. Haynes and Steven L. McKenzie; Louisville: Westminster John Knox, 1999), 230-252.

[20] Knight, "*Wirkungsgeschichte*," 141.

[21] Froehlich, "Biblical Hermeneutics," 9-10; Thiselton, *Hermeneutics: An Introduction*, 320; B. Childs, *The Book of Exodus*, Old Testament Library (Philadelphia: Westminster, 1974), xvi-xvi, 22-24.

## The Absence of Reception History from Evangelical Outlines of the Exegetical Process

It is striking, then, that where Old Testament scholars, especially evangelicals, publish books about the process of exegesis of the kind suited for use as student textbooks, reception history often has little part to play. Even where it is upheld as an interpretive value, it is still usually not incorporated into the formal process of biblical exegesis that is promoted in the text. This remains largely true even in recent editions that have had time to come to terms with what is clearly an important trend in biblical studies overall.[22]

Allow me to illustrate. Douglas Stuart in *Old Testament Exegesis* (4th ed., 2009) says, in advocating the use of a bibliographic index that reaches right back to 1769, "Remember: the old can be gold, and the new is not necessarily true…so do not despise older works."[23] When treating the use of secondary literature later in the book, he expands on this point, recommending that the student access some of the "many great publications from past" whose increasing accessibility is a boon for biblical study.[24] But his no doubt genuine enthusiasm for older works does not translate into any real incorporation of the history of exegesis, let alone reception history more broadly understood, into the process he advocates.[25]

John Hayes and William Holladay offer about the same degree of acknowledgment of reception history in their *Biblical Exegesis: A Beginner's Handbook* (3rd ed., 2009). Expanding on what was a supplementary note to their chapter on historical criticism in the second edition (1988), including a very brief example based on Isa. 7:14,[26] they now gingerly introduce the term 'reception history', noting its usefulness for a deeper sense of the interpretation of a passage in the light of its "historical career."[27] The comments are brief, and that they are embedded in the end of the 'historical criticism' chapter offers a clue as to where the real priorities lie.

---

[22] Thiselton, *Hermeneutics: An Introduction*, 319.

[23] Douglas K. Stuart, *Old Testament Exegesis: A Handbook for Students and Pastors* 4th ed. (Louisville: Westminster John Knox, 2009), 62.

[24] Ibid., 153.

[25] See his outline, ibid., xv-xxi.

[26] John H. Hayes and Carl R. Holladay, *Biblical Exegesis: A Beginner's Handbook*, 2d ed. (London: SCM, 1988), 52.

[27] Carl R. Holladay and John H. Hayes, *Biblical Exegesis: A Beginner's Handbook*, 3rd ed. (Louisville: Westminster John Knox, 2007), 61.

The same is true in Michael Gorman's *Elements of Biblical Exegesis* (rev. ed., 2009). In discussing the final stage of exegesis whereby the student's own exegesis is refined with reference to secondary sources, Gorman declares, "One kind of source that too many exegetes avoid is the work of the great exegetes and preachers of the past—Chrysostom, Augustine, Luther, Wesley, and others. Their literary and theological insights are neglected only to our own detriment. These can be very illuminating sources."[28] The sentiment is doubtless sincere, but this ideal seems to have little weight in the method outlined and could easily be ignored by the student. Jeannine Brown, *Scripture as Communication: Introducing Biblical Hermeneutics* (2007) articulates a well-informed strategy of reconciling concerns with reader, text and author, but again her appended outline of exegesis, while it helpfully includes self-examination of one's presuppositions before and after study of the text, shows no acknowledgment of the history of exegesis.[29]

There is no need to multiply examples further. If even recent works reveal this historical shallowness or light regard for interpreter context, we should perhaps be less surprised when older works treating exegesis fail to show much awareness of the history of exegesis or make reference to reception history. Both conservative and critical presuppositions were capable of predisposing writers not to pay such approaches much attention, because the post-history of a text did not seem to affect its original meaning understood in terms of author intention, the focus of conservative interpretation, or seem relevant to its literary or oral origins, the critical focus. And to be fair, reception theory took some years to catch biblical scholars' attention.[30]

Other writers grant more exposure to reception history or the history of interpretation but do not effectively incorporate either into an exegetical method. Tate, in *Interpreting the Bible: An*

---

[28] Michael J. Gorman, *Elements of Biblical Exegesis: A Basic Guide for Students and Ministers*, rev. ed. (Peabody, MA: Hendrickson, 2009), 170.

[29] Brown, *Scripture as Communication*, 57-74, 275-280.

[30] Reader-oriented approaches are dismissed in Robert B. Chisholm, *From Exegesis to Exposition: A Practical Guide to Using Biblical Hebrew* (Grand Rapids: Baker, 1998), 150-151, 187-191; O. H. Steck, *Old Testament Exegesis: A Guide to the Methodology* ( trans. James D. Nogalski; SBL Resources for Biblical Study, vol. 33; Atlanta: Scholars Press, 1995), 23-26, 159-160. These two authors coming from quite different angles but are both wary of the apparent subjectivism of the new approaches. Noteworthy for a fairly early though sceptical engagement with Gadamer's hermeneutics is Walter C. Kaiser, *Toward an Exegetical Theology: Biblical Exegesis for Preaching and Teaching* (Grand Rapids: Baker Book House, 1984), 17-31.

*Integrated Approach* (3rd ed., 2008), gives significant room to reader-oriented interpretation with a section, "The World In Front of the Text," and treats 'Reception Theory' as one of a series of methodological appendices, but in a way that leaves it looking like just another option in the theoretical smorgasbord, something of a poor cousin to reader-response criticism as mediated by Wolfgang Iser. It is not well integrated into an exegetical method, whereas Tate's 'World in Front of the Text' category offers a rich opportunity for much greater integration of reception history.[31]

Somewhat better integrated is the section devoted to 'Impact History' in the *SCM Studyguide to Biblical Hermeneutics* (2006), a user-friendly guide intended for the popular reader, but which seriously advocates the incorporation the subsequent 'career' of a biblical text into the reader's current perspective on it. However, the authors offer the caveat that this is "a way of looking at the Bible, rather than a method for interpreting it."[32] Moreover, evangelical students are likely to find this work overall so avant-garde and eclectic that their appreciation for the wisdom of this section is liable to be overwhelmed by the difficulties thrown up by the overall work.

There are a few promising signs in one of the evangelical texts on exegesis that I have checked, Craig Broyles' *Interpreting the Old Testament: A Guide for Exegesis* (2001). In his outline of the exegetical process, Broyles places consideration of secondary literature last, maintaining the widely-shared evangelical commitment to the priority of Scripture and the right of private interpretation. But he divides secondary literature into 'current interpretation' and 'history of interpretation', and when he elaborates later, advocates the attempt to transcend our own postmodern and ecclesiastical cultural blind-spots by making reference to "the major periods of church history...and of Jewish interpretation," listing the major categories of each.[33] He does not spend much time expounding this point, but to his credit he has formally incorporated the consideration of these earlier sources into his outline of exegesis. It has made it into the checklist, so to speak, and is thus more likely to be given deliberate

---

[31] W. Randolph Tate, *Interpreting the Bible: An Integrated Approach*, 3rd ed. (Peabody, MA: Hendrickson, 2008), 189-218, 229-230, 317-320.

[32] Holgate and Starr, *Studyguide*, 84. The relevant section occupies pp. 83-88.

[33] Craig C. Broyles, "Interpreting the Old Testament: Principles and Steps," in *Interpreting the Old Testament: A Guide for Exegesis* (ed. Craig C. Broyles; Grand Rapids: Baker Academic, 2001), 23, 61-62.

attention by the student. This is a positive step that needs to be further advanced for reasons I will present below.

## The Background of the Recent Neglect of Christian Reception History

Before I attempt to justify the place of the history of exegesis in our exegetical method, and define how I think reception history in its broader sense ought to be considered, let me flag how the existing deficit in our regard for our interpretive heritage may have arisen. It was not always this way. During the middle millennium of church history, approximately 500-1500 A.D., the most capable of Christian thinkers paid huge regard to their intellectual and spiritual ancestors, such that it has been perceived since as slavishness. At times this was true, but the commentaries and theological works that culminate this trend, those particularly of Catholic interpreters such as Suarez, Petavius, Pererius, à Lapide and Calmet, demonstrate an erudite, encyclopaedic, and indeed critical appropriation of their patristic and medieval heritage, though with a concern to confirm the ultimate coherence of that heritage. Nor did the pre-eminent Protestant role models of Luther and Calvin ignore earlier interpreters, as much as they denied to church tradition the kind of authority or infallibility they attributed to Scripture. In my study of the history of interpretation of the creation week, I found that Luther referred multiple times to the interpretations of Augustine and Hilary of Poitiers, though he urged discretion in their use,[34] and utilised Nicholas of Lyra's late-medieval *Postilla* as a reference work or classroom text.[35]

Calvin likewise cites Augustine most frequently, especially relying on his authority for reinforcement in the *Institutes*, while Calvin's Genesis commentary demonstrates his liberty to disagree with Augustine on such a claim as the latter's instantaneous creation.[36] Calvin and his fellow Reformers also cite numbers of the other

---

[34] "My advice is to read them with discretion." M. Luther, *Lectures on Genesis Chapters 1-5* ( ed. J. Pelikan; trans. George V. Schick; Luther's Works, vol. 1; St. Louis: Concordia, 1958), 61.

[35] Ibid., 3-5, 10, 21-22, 37, 50, 69, etc. See the relevant section in Andrew J. Brown, *The Days of Creation: A History of Christian Interpretation of Genesis 1:1–2:3* (Blandford Forum: Deo Publishing, forthcoming).

[36] John Calvin, *Genesis*, The Geneva Series of Commentaries (London: Banner of Truth, 1965), 78; Johannes Van Oort, "John Calvin and the Church Fathers," in *The Reception of the Church Fathers in the West: From the Carolingians to the Maurists*, ed. Irena Backus (Leiden: E. J. Brill, 1997), 666-667, 671, 682-684.

church fathers appreciatively but also critically and selectively, feeling obliged neither to follow them nor to acknowledge any kind of infallibility in their opinions. Their Catholic contemporaries instead acknowledged a *consensus patrum* or a general agreement of the fathers (and councils) of the church on various doctrines, which consequently demanded submission.[37] Both parties in their different ways and with significantly different motivations continued the vigorous reception of the patristic legacy, with Catholic writers extending their reverence for individual past authorities down as late as Bernard of Clairvaux.[38] Calvin and Luther themselves arguably became authorities of like standing for many subsequent Protestants of their respective traditions.

Tradition, however, was a concept that had fallen out of favour with many Enlightenment thinkers, and the authority of the individual's powers of reason trumped the legacy of a seemingly less mature prior age. This meant the gradual falling away of the cultural authority of both classical Greco-Roman culture and literature and of church hierarchies and heroes. The advent of historical criticism of the Bible, well and truly established by the opening of the nineteenth century in the wake of the pioneering role of J. G. Eichhorn and others, seemed to render pre-critical exegesis of the Bible obsolete, in that it had not and could not have taken literary origins of the text into consideration. A 'devolutionary' view of human civilization that instinctively looked back to classical and biblical models had been replaced by an 'evolutionary' one that now expected that the best in human achievement was to come, and that the highest achievements yet seen were naturally those of the present generation.[39]

The fact that so many of our biblical encyclopaedias, wordbooks and lexica are founded upon nineteenth-century originals demonstrates the abundance and depth of the biblical scholarship that emerged from this kind of confident expectancy. But it is my belief that the negative side of this Enlightenment coin is a kind of present-generation arrogance that dismisses past wisdom and

---

[37] E. P. Meijering, "The Fathers and Calvinist Orthodoxy: Systematic Theology," in *The Reception of the Church Fathers in the West* (ed. I. Backus; Leiden: Brill, 1997), 867; Ralph Keen, "The Fathers in Counter-Reformation Theology in the Pre-Tridentine Period," in *The Reception of the Church Fathers in the West* (ed. I. Backus; Leiden: Brill, 1997), 701.

[38] Keen, "Counter-Reformation Theology," 716.

[39] I have most recently seen these twin terms and the general concept used in Jauss, *Aesthetic Experience and Literary Hermeneutics*, 49.

eventually forgets that it ever really existed. In critical biblical introduction and commentary it appears in the near-absence of consideration of commentary pre-dating the nineteenth or even the twentieth century. More conservative works can similarly be occupied almost exclusively with debates of recent decades, perhaps with the inclusion of key Reformers, but otherwise aspiring to an impartial interpretation of the biblical text with the aid of text-critical and grammatical tools alone.

I personally identify with the *sola scriptura* ideal involved in such approaches. I recognize also that the scientific ideal of inductive reasoning is at work here. We aspire not to allow a pre-determined scheme to dictate what we read out of a biblical text, just as we ought not to permit a theory to skew scientific data, though an interpretive framework or paradigm is indispensable for interpreting such data. The ideal is to observe the data of the text with a methodological objectivity that lets the text say what it will, and then build our biblical theologies cumulatively from the data of such texts. This marries rather well with the Christian (and Protestant) valuing of Scripture as the final arbiter of truth, and applies it at the level of the detail of the text and not merely to Scripture taken as a whole.

We need to temper such ideals with the reality that we do not and cannot actually reason by pure induction in real-world situations. It took thinkers such as Michael Polanyi and Thomas Kuhn in the scientific sphere to remind us that knowledge is communal as well as individual and is brought to the data as well as derived from the data. In literary theory, the epicentre of postmodern philosophies, Gadamer and others have reminded us of the contextual location of the reader. No reader of the Bible is neutral, nor in fact fully equipped with the background information or reading skills necessary for an utterly clear reception of an author's intention in any case; nor do we read free of communal influence. While at its avant-garde fringe postmodern philosophies appear as clique conversations conducted in somewhat self-undermining and certainly obscure terms, Christopher Hall is right to reproduce Craig Blaising's complaint about an evangelical lack of "methodological awareness of the historical nature of interpretation" and to note, "In various ways the postmodern perspective is a helpful correction to the Enlightenment's exaggerated individualism."[40] I do not suggest that we ought to 'adopt' a postmodern perspective, but allow modern and postmodern values to critique one another for the sake of enhancing our own understanding of how we interpret Scripture.

### The Promise of Reception History for Evangelical Interpretation

Reading the seminal texts of reception theory quickly proves that their home context is not biblical studies, but rather epistemology, philosophy of language, literary theory, and art history. For that matter, they are anchored in continental European debates, often have a somewhat rambling, discursive style, and present an arcane face to the uninitiated reader.[41] Not every claim that has been made in reception theory discussion ought to be or can be transferred into biblical studies methods. Even our utilization of reception-historical studies of different biblical texts ought to take note of their theoretical and methodological underpinnings in reception theory and critically evaluate their validity. So what is the wheat and what is the chaff where evangelical hermeneutical purposes are in view?

First, reception theory attempts to reconcile the interpretive concerns of text and historical context. Historical-critical study of the Bible and of other literature was concerned to describe how that literature originated in terms of historical causes, and then what it meant in its original historical context. This could be done in such a thoroughgoing way (such as under the influence of logical positivism) that it left a past document looking necessarily obsolescent in the present, with a meaning related only to an ancient audience. Alternatively, the text might dominate one's interpretation, so that as with the movements of formalism and structuralism, historical concerns were minimized in favour of closely analysing and describing the surface features, or with structuralism the underlying 'structures', of the text.[42] Jauss recognised that texts function in history by meeting, modifying and sometimes refuting audience expectations, expectations which themselves in turn help to shape future texts and their future

---

[40] Christopher Hall, *Reading Scripture with the Church Fathers* (Downers Grove: InterVarsity, 1998), 26-28. He draws the Blaising quote from Mark A. Noll, *The Scandal of the Evangelical Mind* (Grand Rapids: Eerdmans, 1994), 129.

[41] For acknowledgment of this problem of differing spheres of conversation, see Wlad Godzich, Introduction to *Aesthetic Experience and Literary Hermeneutics*, by Hans Robert Jauss (Minneapolis: University of Minnesota Press, 1982).

[42] Jauss, *Toward an Aesthetics of Reception*, 9, 16-18, 70-74, etc.

readers' expectations in turn, in an ongoing feedback cycle. Thus he sought to synthesize formal analysis with historical considerations, specifically those 'in front of' the text or relating to its post-history.

Next, Jauss and Gadamer would both say that every reader has a horizon, a personal context from which he or she sees any text. This prevents absolute objectivity.[43] Gadamer speaks also of the 'historical horizon' that relates to the text's location in its original context, and of interpretation as the process of fusing these two horizons.[44] Jauss speaks instead of the 'horizon' of audience expectation to which the original work responds as contrasted with the horizon of the present reader's experience, meaning that he alters the definition of Gadamer's terms as he adopts them.[45]

Both thinkers have in view a vast series, or better, web of related works and readers constantly feeding back against one another. We might think more simply of three horizons as coming into play whenever we read a biblical text. Under 'historical horizon' we can group together considerations such as author intention, historical setting and posited audience beliefs, values and expectations.[46] In between that horizon and our own reading horizon, incorporating our personal experience, life history, upbringing, community context and so forth, we can identify the horizon of the particular instance of reception history we wish to study, a particular secondary text. This text becomes an illustration both of the original biblical text it expounds and of the hermeneutical method adopted by the author of the time. As we examine both the exposition and the hermeneutics behind it, we learn something of the original horizon, that of the biblical text under study, and turning in the other direction, gain perspective on our own way of

---

[43] Gadamer, *Truth and Method*, 267-269.

[44] Ibid., 272-274. Anthony Thiselton has treated Gadamer's thought at some length: Anthony Thiselton, *The Two Horizons: New Testament Hermeneutics and Philosophical Description with Special Reference to Heidegger, Bultmann, Gadamer, and Wittgenstein* (Exeter: Paternoster, 1980), 293-326. For a simple introduction to the concepts see ibid., 10-17. See also Porter and Robinson, *Hermeneutics*, 74-104.

[45] Jauss, *Toward an Aesthetics of Reception*, 24-28; Parris, *Reception Theory*, 148-154.

[46] By 'historical setting' in this sentence, I am thinking of the point in history when the author has completed the text and offers it for 'public consumption'. If the text is comprised of historical narrative, such as in large sections of our Old Testament historical books and Pentateuch, we also have to reckon with an internal historical setting that pertains, not to the time of writing, but to 'narrative time', the time of the events being reported, which could potentially fall much further back.

approaching and reading biblical texts such as the one being 'received' in the mediating document.

Take for example the Genesis commentary of Denys the Carthusian, (1402/3-1471), one of the late medieval figures most thoroughly acquainted with the church's interpretive heritage. His commentary spends considerable time assessing Augustine's instantaneous creation stance, both to understand biblical creation and to try to discover the vital *consensus patrum* on this matter, so vital to the church's understanding, since Augustine's portrayal of creation seemed so maverick compared to the majority. Using Aristotelian categories derived from Thomas Aquinas, Denys demarcates the 'how' of creation as belonging to the 'accidents' of faith, the negotiable details, whereas the fact of God's creation belongs to the non-negotiable substance. Since Augustine is of one accord with his contemporaries on the latter fact, the consensus remains intact.[47] Denys proceeds to evaluate Augustine's proposition and its rivals, using categories taken from Nicholas of Lyra's then-famous *Postilla,* in terms of contemporary theory about the varieties of matter that may exist and whether any matter can exist before it receives 'form'.[48] Denys finally feels safe in rejecting Augustine's concept of creation on the basis of things said and left unsaid by his own interpretive guide, [Pseudo-] Dionysius the Areopagite, supposedly the convert of Paul mentioned in Acts 17:34, but in fact an anonymous Christian Neoplatonist of the fifth or sixth century A.D.[49]

How does this help us? First, we gain insight into the cultural and intellectual context of late-medieval ecclesiastical interpretation, in Denys' particular monastic, mystical, scholastic style. We gain perspective on the wave of Aristotelian philosophy flavouring late medieval period, and on its scholastic representatives, Albert the Great and Thomas Aquinas. We gain insight into the sheer

---

[47] Dionysius the Carthusian, *Doctoris ecstatici d. Dionysii Cartusiani in Sacram Scripturam commentaria... Tomus I. In Genesim, et Exodum (I-XIX)* (Monstrolii: Cartusiae Sanctae Mariae de Pratis, 1896), 14-16.

[48] Ibid., 16-22.

[49] Ibid., 22. His debt to Pseudo-Dionysius is mentioned in C. G. Thorne, Jr., "Dionysius the Carthusian (1402/3-1471)," in *The New International Dictionary of the Christian Church* (ed. J. D. Douglas; Grand Rapids: Zondervan, 1996), 300-301; F. L. Cross and E. A. Livingstone, eds., *The Oxford Dictionary of the Christian Church*, 2d. rev. ed. (Oxford: Oxford University Press, 1983), 407. The listings on Pseudo-Dionysius are found close by in both dictionaries. See also L. A. Shoemaker, "Denys the Carthusian," in *Historical Handbook of Major Biblical Interpreters* (ed. Donald K. McKim; Downers Grove: InterVarsity, 1998), 95-99.

influence of Augustine's explanation of creation, and through it to the early chapters of Genesis in their own right, all the while seeing, with Denys' help, reasons why we might hesitate before adopting Augustine's interpretation. And we see in the thinking of Denys how the reader's personal horizon affects his reading. The sheer foreignness of a much earlier, but often just as spiritually admirable, interpreter's way of thinking and reading and asking questions can jerk us out of our own rarely-examined interpretive viewpoint, allowing us to 'see the place for the first time'. Perhaps Denys is concerned more than I am with helping Genesis to make sense for Aristotelians. Perhaps that helps me to realize that I am interpreting Genesis to try to make sense of it for scientists, or sceptics, or postmodernists, or fundamentalists. The only truly disinterested reader is the reader who lacks any interest in the text, which may be a solipsism but means that we all come to our Bibles with questions and viewpoints framed by our own experiences and communities. We are just far more used to them than to medieval Aristotelianism and reliance on the church fathers.

We learn how reception functions, therefore, by watching it take place in specific samples of reception history, and thereby become aware of how it works in us. Yet this need not involve submersion in an endless sea of subjectivity, because we also discover that over a long career of reception, discussion of key biblical texts tends to return to similar themes and throw up the same few fundamental stances (e.g. literal, figurative and mystical) toward the text. This encourages us to believe that there are in fact limits to what a biblical text can mean, and if understood as communicative acts, some 'receptions' represent more faithful ways of listening than do others. Augustine explained how the 'Rule of Faith' (*regula fidei*) constituted a kind of 'outer limit' on the diverse range of possible interpretations, and any Christian ultimately seeking an integrated worldview must finally seek some such interpretive focus, if not boundary, of coherence , consensus or compliance (speaking intellectually, socially and spiritually in turn).[50]

---

[50] Augustine, *The Literal Meaning of Genesis* ( trans. John Hammond Taylor; 2 vols; New York: Newman Press, 1982), 44-45 = De Genesi ad litteram 41.21.41; K. E. Greene-McCreight, *Ad Litteram: How Augustine, Calvin, and Barth Read the "Plain Sense" of Genesis 1-3*, Issues in Systematic Theology, vol. 5 (Frankfurt am Main: Lang, 1999), 5-7, 22, 35; John Riches, "Why Write a Reception-Historical Commentary?," *Journal for the Study of the New Testament* 29, no. 3 (2007), 328-331. See also Riches' capable expression late in the section of the value of reception-historical study.

Put another way, Christian interpreters have normally interpreted the Bible in community and with an eye for the Christian community's wellbeing rather than individualistically. To engage with Christian reception history offers the opportunity to participate in the church's exegetical labours over the course of time as well as across ethnic and social boundaries. (In an age when the critical mass of Christianity is becoming non-Western, this skill of crossing our local boundaries is becoming an important one to gain.) The practice of the right kind of reception history is in fact a return to what, until the modern era, has been normal Christian practice, that of learning from the spiritual models that precede us—but perhaps with the benefit of the best insights from recent theorizing about hermeneutics and the dynamics of reception.

But does it represent a defection from the goal of biblical understanding? Stefan Klint in a programmatic article warns that in a reception-historical framework, "The primary object of study will be the work of reception rather than the original biblical text," and thus as a specimen of cultural studies.[51] Whether that is true depends on what we choose to do with reception history. It is simply a tool that we may put to the purpose we believe most worthy. I do not believe its use need eclipse the purpose of our own receiving of a biblical text as not simply as a semiotic web, historical artefact, or merely the communicative act of an ancient author, but a communicative act of God.[52]

## Suggestions for Incorporating Reception History into Evangelical Exegetical Methodology

If it is indeed a virtue to study the reception history of a biblical text, and offers us insights not only into ourselves as readers, but also into given moments in the history of Christian thought and into the texts themselves, it remains to suggest how this ought to be represented in the exegetical process taught to theological students.

I am still enough of a Baconian and an adherent of *sola scriptura* to continue to encourage the inductive approach whereby the student first reads the text him/herself, in the attempt to form initial

---

[51] Stefan Klint, "After Story - a Return to History? Introducing Reception Criticism as an Exegetical Approach," *Studia theologica* 54, no. 2 (2000), 103.

[52] The language of 'communicative act' has epistemological and methodological implications that I lack the room to expound and defend within this article.

impressions relatively uncoloured by others' ideas.[53] My basic exegetical outline for Old Testament study would run as follows:

1. Establish the text.
2. Study the contexts
3. Analyse the content.
4. Synthesize the content.
5. Apply meaning.

Avoiding the temptation to mention everything that such a rump of an outline raises for discussion, I would again observe that normally the consideration of 'secondary literature' appears very late in similar outlines offered by other writers, e.g. Stuart and Broyles. Broyles' inclusion of the text's reception history in this category means that it too appears very late in the exegetical process, almost as an afterthought.[54]

If I must specifically locate consideration of reception history in my outline, it would come late in section 4, 'Synthesize the Content', like so:

a. Identify traditions and themes.
b. Summarize the passage.
c. Explain the passage in its literary context.
d. Explain its point of view and original purpose.
e. Identify Old Testament inner-biblical links and allusions.
f. Identify New Testament appropriation, along with ancient extrabiblical reception to this point, e.g. Apocrypha, Pseudepigrapha, Qumran.
g. Explain the passage in the context of a whole-Bible biblical theology.
h. Uncover examples of post-biblical reception, especially Christian, but also Jewish, Gnostic, secular, etc., and both ancient and modern.

I would hope then that the primary reception-historical stage, step (h), might lead naturally into the first sub-point of Stage 5, 'Apply Meaning', which is (a) 'Consider transferability [of the meaning] to our present', on the way to summing up and 'packaging' the meaning found for one's anticipated audience.

---

[53] My way of encouraging the student to acknowledge the inevitable 'colouring' of his or her 'personal horizon' is to include within Step 2, 'Study the Contexts', a deliberate look at the 'Personal Context' as well as historical, socio-cultural and literary contexts of the text in question.

[54] Stuart, *Old Testament Exegesis*, xxi; Broyles, "Principles and Steps," 23.

However, neither secondary literature generally nor reception-history examples in particular can or should be quarantined to the latest stages of the exegetical process. I would envisage that not only primary language tools, but also commentaries and even interpretive viewpoints from reception history might begin to play a part even in the analysis stage. Then as exegesis moves towards synthesis and application, examples of reception of the text ancient and modern, sympathetic and sceptical, sacred and secular, and from standard commentary to popular culture, might offer stimulating examples of how to read and apply the text concerned, and very likely how not to as well (which implies retaining the right to make value judgments about the various readings encountered, primarily on theological and biblical grounds).

But this risks becoming another vain ambition, the kind of rosy hope that real-world time constraints will quickly kill off. The busy exegete of whatever stripe has his or her hands full simply becoming acquainted with the passage. Rare would be the person in the church circles I move in who would even attempt to browse a biblical text in its original language prior to preaching it, let alone looking engaging in any scholarly research into it. But this is a question of mentality. One thing many preachers and teachers do find time for is to turn to their favourite lightweight application-style commentary for an idea or two. It is not much harder to consult, for instance, Calvin's reprinted commentaries, or sample patristic views in the *Ancient Christian Commentary* series, or consult the Christian Classics Ethereal Library online, or Google for references to our biblical text in artworks or popular culture. It is a matter of looking beyond the last forty years, and sometimes beyond the commentary genre, for insights. There will not be time to pick out more than a few samples, but a few will be better than none, and those few samples may well offer surprising or stimulating perspectives on the meaning impregnated in and/or imputed to the original text. Encountering such examples might begin to build into the student's perspective on the biblical text a growing and needful historical as well as hermeneutical sensitivity that can buttress his or her theological aptitude.

A final example comes to mind. I recently taught Genesis 2-3 in an Old Testament survey subject. The tree of life that features in those chapters is a potent symbol suggesting multiple connotations. Turning to the first volume of the *Ancient Christian Commentary on Scripture* edited by Andrew Louth, I find that it led Jerome to think of Christ as the source of wisdom, while Gregory of Nazianzus characterized the cross of Golgotha as its New Testament antitype, a new, redemptive 'tree of life'. But just last night, I saw a police drama on television dealing with a neo-pagan, occult theme, and it featured a medallion engraved with a fertility-tree symbol, reminding me of this curious symbolic intersection of Christianity and paganism, ancient and modern. Given that the tree of life had a potent afterlife in Christian iconography through the Middle Ages and onward,[55] here perhaps was an interesting entry point for discussing the meaning of one suggestive element of this Genesis text, and thence its biblical-theological significance, with conversation partners both within and outside of the church community.

---

[55] Jennifer O'Reilly, "The Trees of Eden in Mediaeval Iconography," in *A Walk in the Garden: Biblical, Iconographical and Literary Images of Eden* (ed. P. Morris and D. Sawyer; Sheffield: Sheffield Academic, 1992), 170-180.

# Paul the Law and the Spirit

Colin Kruse

Melbourne School of Theology

Abstract:

*On first reading Paul's letters to the Galatians and the Romans especially one might gain the impression that Paul's attitude to the Mosaic law was largely negative, and that with the coming of the Spirit following the death and resurrection of Christ there was no further place for the law in the lives of belie vers. However, the material surveyed in this article reveals that Paul's teaching about the law and the Spirit is more complex than that. While he teaches that the law condemns and kills whereas the Spirit gives life, and that believers need to be freed from the law to 'bear fruit for God', yet, paradoxically he insists that 'the just requirement of the law' is fulfilled in those who walk by the Spirit. While the law does not function as the regulatory norm for believers it is nevertheless their Scripture that bears witness to Christ and is a source of instruction for godly living when read paradigmatically in the light of the gospel.*

## Introduction

The purpose of this essay is to explore the apostle Paul's teaching concerning the relationship between the Mosaic law and the Spirit of God following the coming of Christ. However, lest we fall into the trap of assuming that Paul's emphasis upon the role of the Spirit indicates a wholly negative attitude on his part towards the law, it is necessary to document briefly the many facets of the apostle's teaching about the law, noting both its positive and the negative aspects.

Paul taught that the possession of the law was one of the great privileges of the Jews (Rom 2:18-20; 9:4-5). It was introduced for a limited period of time only—from Moses to Christ (Rom 7:1-4; 9:4; 10:4; 2 Cor 3:11; Eph 2:14-16) and one of its functions was to make sin known (Rom 7:7). While the law is holy, just, good and spiritual (Rom 7:12-14), it became the unwilling ally of sin thus compounding human slavery to sin (Rom 7:9-11; 1 Cor 15:56). It cannot give life (Gal 3:21-22)—in fact it brings condemnation and death (2 Cor 3:7, 9). It does not annul the promise God gave to

Abraham (Gal 3:15-18), nor is it contrary to that promise (Gal 3:21-22). The law functions as a witness to the gospel of Christ (Rom 3:21; 4:1-25; 10:5-8; 2 Cor 3:14-15). One of its purposes was to restrain sin until the coming of Christ (Gal 3:23-24; 4:1-5), and thereafter it has no further role as a regulatory norm for those who believe in him (Gal 2:15-21).

Nevertheless, Paul has a lot to say about the law and the believer. He emphasises strongly that believers are free from the law as a regulatory norm (Rom 6:14; 7:1, 5-6; 1 Cor 9:20-21; 2 Cor 11:24; Gal 2:3-5, 11-14; 3:23—4:5; 5:1, 18; Col 2:16-17), and that they need to stand fast in this freedom (Gal 5:1) so as to bear fruit for God (Rom 7:4-6). Gentiles who place themselves under the law fall from grace and become alienated from Christ (Gal 5:2-4). Paul used the law to instruct believers, especially in regard to its testimony to the gospel (Rom 1:2; 3:21; Gal 3:6, 8, 16; 4:21, 30), and as a guide for Christian living when read paradigmatically in the light of Christ (1 Cor 5:6-8; 9:8-12, 13-14; 10:1-11; 11:7-10; 14:20-25, 34-35; 2 Cor 6:14—7:1; 8:13-15; 1 Tim 5:17-18; 2 Tim 3:14-17). The apostle expected the law to find fulfilment in the lives of believers (Rom 8:3-4) as they observed the law of Christ (Rom 13:8-10; Gal 5:14; 6:2). He also expected those who understood their freedom from the law (especially Gentile believers) to respect the convictions of those who did not understand that freedom (usually Jewish believers) (Rom 14:1-6), and even to forego their own freedom so as to enhance evangelistic efforts among Jewish people (Rom 14:13-18).[1]

Whilst the apostle Paul had many positive things to say about the law, nevertheless, a very significant change took place in his understanding of its role with the advent of Christ, his death, resurrection and sending of the Holy Spirit. We will keep an eye out for the impact of the coming of the Spirit upon Paul's understanding of the role of the law as we examine those passages in the Pauline corpus where the law and the Spirit are brought together by the apostle.[2] These can be conveniently grouped under the following headings.

---

[1] For a more detailed treatment of Paul's attitude to the law see, Colin G. Kruse, *Paul, the Law and Justification* (Leicester: Apollos, 1996), especially the summaries on pages 107-109, 112-114, 144-146, 158-160, 240, 242-243, 247-249, 271-272.

[2] Unless otherwise indicated all Scripture quotations are taken from the NRSV.

## The Role of the Law and the Spirit Contrasted

In 2 Corinthians 3:7-11 there is an implied contrast between the role of the law in ministry under the old covenant and the role of the Spirit in ministry under the new covenant:

> Now if the ministry of death, chiselled in letters on stone tablets, came in glory so that the people of Israel could not gaze at Moses' face because of the glory of his face, a glory now set aside, how much more will the ministry of the Spirit come in glory? For if there was glory in the ministry of condemnation, much more does the ministry of justification abound in glory! Indeed, what once had glory has lost its glory because of the greater glory; for if what was set aside came through glory, much more has the permanent come in glory!

This passage is part of a longer section, 2 Corinthians 3:7-18, in which Paul seeks to neutralize any residual doubts his readers may have had about him, and also to carry the attack to the 'false apostles' already present and voicing their criticisms of him in Corinth during the period of the crisis reflected in 2 Corinthians 1--7.[3] The view that 2 Corinthians 3:7-18 does have such a polemic purpose has been supported by several modern commentators.[4] Our passage is an exposition of Exodus 34:29-32 (which tells of the glory that attended the giving of the law, a glory reflected in the shining face of Moses that struck fear into the hearts of the Israelites). Paul recognizes that the old covenant was accompanied by splendour, but using a rabbinic method of exegesis (from the lesser to the greater) he argues that the new covenant is accompanied by far greater splendour. The superiority of new covenant ministry is argued on three counts. The ministry of the Spirit is more splendid than the ministry of death, the ministry of justification is more splendid than that of condemnation, and the permanent ministry is more splendid than one that has been set aside.[5].

---

[3] *Cf.* Colin G. Kruse, "The Relationship between the Opposition to Paul Reflected in 2 Corinthians 1-7 and 10-13," *EvQ* 61 (1989), 195-202, 199-202.

[4] So, *e.g.* Dieter Georgi, *The Opponents of Paul in Second Corinthians* (Philadelphia: Fortress, 1986), 254, 260-261; William J. Dalton, "Is the Old Covenant Abrogated (2 Cor 3.14)?" *AusBR* 35 (1987), 84-94, 90-91. Victor Paul Furnish, *II Corinthians* (AB 32a; New York: Doubleday, 1984), 225, recognizes that polemic concerns surface in 2 Cor 2:17; 3:1, 7-18 and 4:1-2, but argues that 2 Cor 3:7-18 is not fundamentally polemic. Ralph P. Martin, *2 Corinthians* (WBC 40, Waco, Texas: Word, 1986), 66, speaks of a polemic undertone.

[5] E. P. Sanders, *Paul, the Law, and the Jewish People* (London: SCM, 1985), 139, notes that the neuter participle καταργούμενον ('set aside') in 3:11 refers to the law itself, not the glory with which it came (which would require a feminine participle). The temporary nature of the law has been the subject of some discussion in recent periodical literature. Peter von der Osten-

The primary instrument of the ministry of the old covenant was the law—chiselled in letters on stone tablets (2 Cor 3:7)—and in this passage Paul implies that it is the law that condemns and kills, and though attended with glory when given on Sinai, its role was temporary. The primary instrument of the ministry of the new covenant is the Spirit, and Paul implies the Spirit gives life.[6]

Paul describes the law 'carved in letters on stone' as 'the ministry' of death'. This is best understood in the light of Romans 7:10 where the apostle says, 'the very commandment which promised life, proved to be death to me.' Although Leviticus 18:5 may promise life to those who keep the law, Paul knew that no one does so in fact, and that the law pronounces the verdict of death over the

---

sacken, "Geist im Buchstaben. Vom Glanz des Mose und des Paulus," *EvT* 41 (1981), 230-235, 231, claims: 'Nicht nur wohnt dem Dienst des Mose Doxa inne, es ist mit dieser Doxa auch nach Paulus noch keineswegs vorbei; "sie *wird* beseitigt"--viermal verwendet Paulus präsentische Formen, kein einziges Mal solche des Prätertium (vv. 7, 11, 13, 14)—nicht etwa, dass sie beseitigt *worden* wäre.' While Osten-Sacken's observations about the use of the present tense are correct, he appears to overlook the fact that Paul could have been speaking of a glory which had not yet faded only because he was presenting the situation as it appeared in Moses day, not as it had become following the Christ event. Dalton, "Is the Old Covenant Abrogated?", 90-91, says that the old covenant is still in force, arguing that Paul believed 'the transitory nature of Moses' glory is a sign of the passing relationship of the Law *with Gentiles* (italics added).' He appeals to Romans 9-11 (esp. 11:25-32) as evidence that the old covenant is still in force for Israel. However, Rom 11:25-32 does not say that the old covenant is still in force, but that God's gift and calling in respect of Israel are irrevocable. This means that God's promises to them will be honoured if they do not persist in their unbelief (11:23). Unbelief in this context must be understood to mean rejection of the gospel, which indicates that even the Jews must now relate to God under the terms of the new covenant. Morna D. Hooker, "Beyond the Things that are Written? St Paul's Use of Scripture," *NTS* 27 (1981), 295-309, 304, argues that the law was temporary in so far as its offer of life to those who fulfil its demands has been superseded with the coming of Christ, but that the law is abiding in so far as it is a witness to Christ. This seems to be a satisfactory approach, giving due weight to the various nuances of the text itself. However, it should be added that the law has an ongoing role in ethical instruction as long as it is read paradigmatically in the light of Christ.

[6] Randal C. Gleason, "Paul's Covenantal Contrasts in 2 Corinthians 3:1-11," *BSac* 154 (1997), 61-79, 70-76 notes five interpretations of the γράμμα/πνεῦμα (letter/spirit) contrast: literal and spiritual senses of Scripture; the text written and the Spirit as interpreter; the legalistic misuse of the law and the Holy Spirit; outward conformity versus inward obedience to the Mosaic law; and the old covenant and the new covenant. Gleason opts for the last of these as the correct one. Karl Kertelge, "Letter and Spirit in 2 Corinthians 3," in *Paul and the Mosaic law* (ed. James D. G. Dunn; Grand Rapids: Eerdmans, 2001), 117-130, 128, comments: 'We cannot simply understand the antithesis of letter and spirit in 3:6 in terms of two opposing and exclusive orders of salvation. Instead, they point to the life-giving power of the Spirit at work in the gospel, which overcomes the death-dealing power of the law. The demonstration of the Spirit in the gospel erases the death-dealing power of the law, but not the (Mosaic) law as such. This law finds it new expression as the 'law of Christ' (Gal 6:2) which is binding on Christians.' Michael Winger, "The law of Christ," *NTS* 46 (2000), 537-546, 544, suggests that the law of Christ refers 'to the way Christ exercises his lordship over those called by him', and this means that 'it is necessary for those who are "of Christ" (5.25) to live in a way that is organised by the Spirit'.

transgressor. Unlike the law 'chiselled in letters on stone tablets' that could not enable a person to fulfil its own demands, the Spirit given under the new covenant enlivens people and causes them to walk in the way of God's commandments (*cf.* Ezek 36:27).

## Redeemed from the Curse of the Law to Receive the Gift of the Spirit

Two passages in Galatians speak of the need for the redemption of Jewish people from under the law and its curse so that they may receive the gift of the Spirit:

> Christ redeemed us from the curse of the law by becoming a curse for us—for it is written, 'Cursed is everyone who hangs on a tree'—in order that in Christ Jesus the blessing of Abraham might come to the Gentiles, so that we might receive the promise of the Spirit through faith (Gal 3:13-14).

> But when the fullness of time had come, God sent his Son, born of a woman, born under the law, in order to redeem those who were under the law, so that we might receive adoption as children. And because you are children, God has sent the Spirit of his Son into our hearts, crying, 'Abba! Father!' (Gal 4:4-6)

Galatians 4:4-6 speaks in general terms of the need of redemption for those 'under the law' (*i.e.* Jews), but Galatians 3:13-14 is more specific speaking of the need for redemption from the 'curse' of the law. In this case the apostle clearly connects redemption from the curse of the law and the reception of the Spirit.

'The curse of the law' brings to mind immediately the blessings and curses attaching to YHWH's covenant with Israel. In Deuteronomy 11:26-28 Moses says to Israel: ' See, I am setting before you today a blessing and a curse: the blessing, if you obey the commandments of the LORD your God that I am commanding you today; and the curse, if you do not obey the commandments of the LORD your God, but turn from the way that I am commanding you today, to follow other gods that you have not known.' The curses that would befall a disloyal and disobedient Israel are described in detail in Deuteronomy 28:15-68, and they include suffering God's curse in city and field, in basket and kneading bowl, in the fruit of the womb and of the ground, and of cattle and flocks. In addition Israel would experience panic and destruction, pestilence, diseases, blight and mildew, drought, defeat at the hand of their enemies, blindness and confusion of mind. They would plant vineyards and olive trees but not enjoy their produce. Others would eat the fruit of their vineyards, seize their cattle and flocks, and lie with their women. Aliens living among them would dominate them. A nation from far away would descend upon them, consuming their produce and livestock, besieging their towns with all the attendant horrors—they would be reduced to cannibalism. The Lord would bring upon them maladies and afflictions until they were destroyed. And though they were once as numerous as the stars of heaven they would be left few in number. Israel would be taken into exile and serve other kings and other gods.

The ultimate expression of the curse was exile, a fate suffered by the northern kingdom of Israel at the hands of the Assyrians in the eighth century BC, and by the southern kingdom of Judah at the hands of the Babylonians in the sixth century BC. The question this raises is whether Paul thought of the curse of the law in terms of exile, or as been suggested, in terms of Israel's subjection to Roman occupying forces. Was the occupation a sign that Israel was still suffering the curse of the law? And if so, did Paul understand the death of Christ as effecting Israel's redemption from the curse, so that God's blessings promised long ago to Abraham might now flow to Israel and then on to the Gentiles, blessings Paul understood to include reception of the promised Holy Spirit.[7] There is a certain logic to this approach, but it is problematic because Paul never speaks of Roman occupation as the result of the curse of God because of Israel's sin (and neither did Jesus). Nor does he speak of redemption as release from the Roman occupation. When Christ became a curse for us he did so by enduring death upon the cross, suffering there the divine wrath towards human sin. That he did this 'for us' indicates that the curse of the law from which 'we' need redemption involved experiencing that same wrath ourselves.

In Galatians 3:13-14 and 4:4-6, then, Paul says that God redeemed those under the law (Jews) from the curse of the law (exposure to God's wrath) with the result that when Jews believe in God's Son

---

[7] N. T. Wright, *The Climax of the Covenant: Christ and the Law in Pauline Theology* (Edinburgh: T& T Clark, 1991), 140-14, argues that the curse of the law is to be understood in terms of Israel's ongoing exile. 'Deuteronomy 27—30', he says, 'is all about exile and restoration, *understood as* covenant judgment and covenant renewal.' On the basis of 'many sources' in the Qumran documents (*e.g.* CD 1:5-8), he argues that some first-century Jews at least believed the exile still continued, and 'as long as Pilate and Herod were in charge of Palestine, Israel was still under the curse of Deuteronomy 29'. Wright asserts that Gal 1:4 (Paul's reference to 'the present evil age') is enough to show that Paul thought in this way. Mark A. Seifrid, "Blind Alleys in the Controversy over the Paul of History," *TynBul* 45 (1994), 73-95, 86-89, draws attention to several Jewish texts which indicate there was a range of views concerning the status of Israel, and not all of these reflect the view that all Israel was still in exile.

they would be adopted as God's children, and receive the promise of the Spirit.[8] The promise came first to the Jews (on the day of Pentecost), and then to the Gentiles as the gospel was taken to them.[9]

## The Spirit Experienced Independently of Obedience to the Law

The apostle Paul insisted not only that the Jews had to be redeemed from the curse of the law so that they might receive the promise of the Spirit and so that this promise might extend to the Gentiles, he also insisted that the Gentiles received the Spirit without performing works of the law. In Galatians 3:1-5 he says:

> You foolish Galatians! Who has bewitched you? It was before your eyes that Jesus Christ was publicly exhibited as crucified! The only thing I want to learn from you is this: Did you receive the Spirit by doing the works of the law or by believing what you heard? Are you so foolish? Having started with the Spirit, are you now ending with the flesh? Did you experience so much for nothing?—if it really was for nothing. Well then, does God supply you with the Spirit and work miracles among you by your doing the works of the law, or by your believing what you heard?

This passage is part of Paul's extended argument that Gentile believers are accepted as Abraham's children, true members of the people of God, and justified by faith without works of the law just as Abraham was. In Galatians 3:1-5 Paul supports this argument by appeal to the Galatians' experience of the Spirit. He asks the Galatians five questions to make his point, and two of these are pertinent to our study. First, he asks: 'The only thing I want to learn from you is this: Did you receive the Spirit by doing the works of the law or by believing what you heard (ἐξ ἀκοῆς πίστεως)'[10] In this

---

[8] While many modern commentators take the 'we' who are redeemed to be inclusive (Jews and Gentiles), there are a number who argue, rightly in my view, for the exclusive option (Jews), so *e.g.* F. F. Bruce, *The Epistle of Paul to the Galatians: A Commentary on the Greek Text* (NIGTC; Exeter: Paternoster, 1980), 193, Richard N. Longenecker, *Galatians* (WBC 41; Dallas, TX: Word, 1990), 164; T. L. Donaldson, "The 'Curse of the Law' and the Inclusion of the Gentiles: Galatians 3.13-14," *NTS* 32 (1986), 94-112, 95-99.

[9] *Cf. e.g.* Acts 10:44-46; 11:15-18.

[10] ἐξ ἀκοῆς πίστεως has usually been construed by commentators to mean 'by faith in what was heard', *i.e.* the gospel (so *e.g.* Heinrich Schlier, *Der Brief an die Galater* (KEK; Göttingen: Vandenhoeck und Ruprecht, 1962), 122; E. P. Sanders, *Paul and Palestinian Judaism: A Comparison of Patterns of Religion* (London: SCM, 1977), 482-483; Hans Dieter Betz, *Galatians: A Commentary on Paul's Letter to the Churches in Galatia* (Hermeneia; Philadelphia: Fortress, 1979), 133; Bruce, *Galatians*, 149; Longenecker, *Galatians*, 102-103). Richard B. Hays, *The Faith of Jesus Christ. An Interpretation of the Narrative Substructure of Galatians 3:1—4:11* (SBLDS

context to ask whether they had received the Spirit by works of law or by the hearing of faith, was tantamount to asking whether they had been justified by works of law or by the hearing of faith. The expected answer was, of course, we received the Spirit 'by believing what was heard', and the corollary being our justification is also independent of our doing works prescribed by the law. Underlying Paul's argument here is the assumption that the initial reception of the Spirit by Gentile believers was independent of their doing works prescribed by the law.

Second, Paul asks: 'Well then, does God supply you with the Spirit and work miracles among you by your doing the works of the law, or by your believing what you heard?' (Gal 3:5). The reference to the supplying of the Spirit (by God) is probably an allusion to the Galatians' conversion when they received the Spirit initially, and the reference to the working of miracles (by God) is probably a reference to the ongoing work of the Spirit among them. If this is the case, this question picks up the two different aspects of the Galatians' experience of the Spirit (the initial and the ongoing). What Paul is stressing is that neither the initial experience of the Spirit nor his ongoing activity among believers is dependent upon their doing the works of the law.[11]

## Freed from the Law to Serve in the New Way of the Spirit

One striking thing Paul says about the law is that people need to be freed from its demands so that they might walk in the Spirit and bear fruit for God. The most important text in this regard is Romans 7:4-6:

> In the same way, my friends, you have died to the law through the body of Christ, so that you may belong to another, to him who has been raised from the dead in order that we may bear fruit for God. While we were living in the flesh, our sinful passions, aroused by the law, were at work in our members to bear fruit for death. But now we

---

56, Chico, Ca.: Scholars Press, 1983), 143-149, 197-198, prefers to interpret ἀκοὴ πίστεως as the proclaimed message that evokes faith. However, Sam K. Williams, "The Hearing of Faith: Ἀκοὴ πίστεως in Galatians 3," *NTS* 35 (1989), 82-93, 90 suggests that 'the hearing of faith' means 'the hearing which Christians call faith'. This was essentially how J. B. Lightfoot, *Saint Paul's Epistle to the Galatians* (London: Macmillan, 1902), 135, preferred to read it as well. G. Walter Hansen, *Abraham in Galatians: Epistolary and Rhetorical Contests* (JSNTSup 29; Sheffield: JSOT, 1989), 110-111, argues for 'hearing with faith', by which he means the human activity of believing. This, he argues, is supported by the inferences Paul draws in Gal 3:7 from his citation of Gen. 15:6 in Gal 3:6.

[11] *Cf.* Longenecker, *Galatians*, 105-106.

are discharged from the law, dead to that which held us captive, so that we are slaves not under the old written code but in the new life of the Spirit.

Romans 7:4-6 is part of a longer passage Romans 7:1-6 that foreshadows what will be argued in more detail in Romans 7:7-8:13, and accordingly its programmatic nature has been noted by a number of scholars.[12] In particular, Romans 7:5 foreshadows Romans 7:7-25 where life in the flesh and under the law is depicted, and Romans 7:6 foreshadows Romans 8:1-13 where freedom and service in 'the new life of the Spirit' is explained.[13]

Paul addresses 'those who know the law' (Rom 7:1),[14] reminding them that 'the law is binding on a person only during that person's lifetime'. He reinforces his reminder with an analogy based upon marriage law (Rom 7:2-4), arguing that just as the death of a husband discharges his widow from any obligation to observe the law that bound her to him, so likewise the death of Christ discharges believers from their obligation to obey the law (of Moses).[15] Paul's argument raises difficulties because of the lack of correspondence between the analogy itself and what he seeks to show from it. He asserts that 'the law is binding on a person only during that person's lifetime' (Rom 7:1), and in his application of the analogy he makes the same point: believers having died (in Christ) are discharged from their obligation to the law (Rom 7:4a).

---

[12] *Cf., e.g.* Bruce Morrison and John Woodhouse, "The Coherence of Romans 7:1—8:8," *Reformed Theological Review* 47 (1988), 8-16, 14; S. Voorwinde, "Who is the 'Wretched Man' in Romans 7:24?" *Vox Reformata* 54 (1990), 11-26, 21.

[13] So Voorwinde, "Who is the 'Wretched Man' in Romans 7:24?" 21.

[14] This expression taken on its own could refer simply to people who know about any system of marriage law, but in the context Paul would seem to have in mind the Mosaic law from which, he argues, believers have been set free. Therefore the expression has significance for discussions about the readership and the purpose of Romans. However, it is not as helpful to us in this connection as it might first appear because it is susceptible to several interpretations. Within the overall context of Romans 'those who know the law' could refer to: (i) Christian Jews (who made up part of the Roman church); (ii) Gentile Christians who had been formerly proselytes; (iii) Gentile Christians who had been formerly loosely attached to the synagogue as God-fearers; (iv) Gentile Christians who had gained an understanding of the law/OT since they joined the church.

[15] Luzia Sutter Rehmann, "The Doorway into Freedom: The Case of the 'Suspected Wife' in Romans 7.1-6," *JSNT* 79 (2000), 91-104, 97-102 sees the background to Rom 7:1-6 in Num 5:29-30: 'This is the law in cases of jealousy, when a wife, while under her husband's authority, goes astray and defiles herself, or when a spirit of jealousy comes on a man and he is jealous of his wife; then he shall set the woman before the LORD, and the priest shall apply this entire law to her.' The law was that the woman be required to drink the *sotah* (the bitter water) to prove here innocence. However, according to *m. Sotah* 4.2, if her husband died before she drank it then she was free from the requirement to drink the *sotah*, that is free from the law of the husband, and she would still be able to receive her *ketubah* (dowry).

However, in the analogy itself (Rom 7:2-3) it is not the death of the wife that frees her from the law binding her to her husband (which we would expect and which Paul could have said to make this point), but it is the death of the husband that frees her. The reason why Paul did not construct his analogy with the sort of exact correspondence that we might expect is that he wanted to use the analogy to make an additional point. Not only did he want to show that the death of believers in Christ frees them from obligation to the law, but also that it frees them to belong to Christ and 'bear fruit to God' (Rom 7:4b). For the analogy to be able to be used to make this additional point the wife must remain alive in order to be able to marry another man, and so it must be the death of the husband which discharges her from the marriage law. Paul does not seem to have been concerned about the lack of exact correspondence (as we, his modern readers are), being satisfied with an analogy in which death (albeit the husband's and not the wife's) frees from the law so that the one freed can then belong to another.[16]

This analogy and its application constitute one of the clearest expressions of Paul's belief that believers (Jews as well as Gentiles) are completely freed from all obligations to the Mosaic law as a regulatory norm. Like a person who has died, they have been discharged from all obligations to the law. Underlying this notion of freedom from the law is the assumption that the period of the law has come to an end with the coming of Christ.

For Paul this death to the law's demands has two positive outcomes that can be seen in Romans 7:5-6. In Romans 7:5 he implies that believers' release from the law means they may escape the dilemma of having their sinful passions 'aroused by the law' (a dilemma

---

[16] J. A. Ziesler, *Paul's Letter to the Romans* (London/ Philadelphia: SCM/Trinity, 1989), 174-175, notes that the analogy makes one straightforward point ('legal obligations are removed by death'), and that attempts to work out the illustration in detail run into confusion. Joyce A. Little, "Paul's Use of Analogy: A Structural Analysis of Romans 7:1-6," *CBQ* 46 (1984), 982-90, 90, discusses the inconsistencies in Paul's use of the analogy. She disagrees with Dodd's conclusion that 'he [Paul] lacks the gift for sustained illustration of ideas through concrete images (though he is capable of a brief illuminatory metaphor). It is probably a defect of imagination.' Little argues instead that 'the defect Paul suffers from in the writing of this passage is, if anything, an excess of imagination which propels him through the above-noted succession of ideas so rapidly that he has neither the time nor the opportunity to bring his images to completion.' She adds that it is not certain that Paul could have brought his images to completion, even if he had been so inclined. But cp. John D. Earnshaw, "Reconsidering Paul's Marriage Analogy in Romans 7.1-4," *NTS* 40 (1994), 69-88, 72, who argues that 'Paul's marriage analogy is properly understood only when *the wife's first marriage is viewed as illustrating the believer's union with Christ in his death and her second marriage is viewed as illustrating the believer's union with Christ in his resurrection*'.

which he expounds in Rom 7:7-25). In verse 6 he says that believers' release from the law enables them to live 'the new life of the Spirit' (something he expounds in Rom 8:1-13). The implied contrast between the law and the Spirit is that under the law sin is aroused and so people are doomed to bear fruit to death, whereas under the reign of the Spirit they are free to bear fruit for God.

The other important passage in which Paul connects the need for people to be free from the law's demands with life in the Spirit is found in Galatians 5:16-18. In this passage the apostle speaks of the tension between the flesh and the Spirit in the life of believers and urges his readers to walk by the Spirit:

> Live by the Spirit, I say, and do not gratify the desires of the flesh. For what the flesh desires is opposed to the Spirit, and what the Spirit desires is opposed to the flesh; for these are opposed to each other, to prevent you from doing what you want. But if you are led by the Spirit, you are not subject to the law.

These verses are a part of the larger section, Galatians 5:13-18, where Paul urges his readers not to use their freedom from the law as an opportunity for self-indulgence (Gal 5:13). They are to live by the Spirit and not gratify the desires of the flesh.[17] What is involved in these two different life-styles Paul himself spells out in the section that follows (Gal 5:19-24) where he contrasts the 'works of the flesh' (Gal 5:19-21) with the 'fruit of the Spirit' (Gal 5:22-24).

In Galatians 5:16-18 Paul reminds his readers of the conflict between the Spirit and the flesh: 'For what the flesh desires is opposed to the Spirit, and what the Spirit desires is opposed to the flesh; for these are opposed to each other, to prevent you from doing what you want' (Gal 5:17). The next verse comes as something of a surprise. We might have expected Paul to say that if people are led by the Spirit they will not fulfil the desires of the flesh. However, what he says is not that, but rather, 'if you are led by the Spirit, you are not subject to the law' (Gal 5:18). The implication of this surprising statement is that being free from the

---

[17] Walter Bo Russell, "Does the Christian Have 'Flesh' in Gal 5:13-26," *JETS* 36 (1993), 179-187, 186-187, says, 'I believe that σάρξ and πνεῦμα have become theological abbreviations in Paul's argument that represent the two competing identities of the people of God in Galatia. The "flesh community" (Judaizers) is a community identified with the Mosaic era and is therefore a community identified and characterized by a person bodily in his or her frailty and transitoriness and not indwelt by God's Spirit.... By contrast the "Spirit community" is a community identified and characterized by a person bodily aided and enabled by God's presence and also bodily liberated from sin's dominion, a person experiencing the full liberation of Jesus' death and resurrection.'

law is intimately connected with overcoming the desires of the flesh.

This is contrary to the fears that probably haunted many Jewish believers (including the Judaizers) when they heard about the influx of Gentiles into the church as a result of Paul's mission. They feared that the Gentile believers who were not under the law would quickly succumb to the desires of the flesh. But Paul implies that not being under the law had the opposite effect. It enabled people to resist the desires of the flesh. Longenecker sums up the matter well:

> The Judaizers had undoubtedly argued that only two options existed for Galatian Christians: either (1) a lifestyle governed by Torah, or (2) a lifestyle giving way to license, such as formerly characterized their lives as Gentiles apart from God. The Christian gospel, however, as Paul proclaimed it, has to do with a third way of life that is distinct from both nomism and libertinism--not one that takes a middle course between the two, as many try to do in working out a Christian lifestyle on their own, but that is "a highway above them both" (Burton, *Galatians*, 302). The antidote to license in the Christian life is not laws, as the Judaizers argued, but openness to the Spirit and being guided by the Spirit. For being 'in Christ' means neither nomism nor libertinism, but a new quality of life based in and directed by the Spirit.[18]

## The Law Written on Human Hearts by the Spirit

The prophets Jeremiah and Ezekiel predicted a time when the law of God would be written on the hearts of God's people:

> The days are surely coming, says the LORD, when I will make a new covenant with the house of Israel and the house of Judah. It will not be like the covenant that I made with their ancestors when I took them by the hand to bring them out of the land of Egypt—a covenant that they broke, though I was their husband, says the LORD. But this is the covenant that I will make with the house of Israel after those days, says the LORD: I will put my law within them, and I will write it on their hearts; and I will be their God, and they shall be my people (Jer 31:31-33).

> A new heart I will give you, and a new spirit I will put within you; and I will remove from your body the heart of stone and give you a

---

[18] *Galatians*, 246. It may be asked whether there is evidence to justify the confidence with which Longenecker says that the Judaizers saw things as he describes them here. But this aside, Longenecker's comments seem to be right on target.

heart of flesh. I will put my spirit within you, and make you follow my statutes and be careful to observe my ordinances (Ezek 36:26-27).

In Romans 2:14-16 Paul appears to say that these prophecies find fulfilment in the lives of Gentile believers:

> When Gentiles, who do not possess the law, do instinctively what the law requires, [or better: Gentiles who by birth do not posses the law, do what the law requires] these, though not having the law, are a law to themselves. They show that what the law requires is written on their hearts, to which their own conscience also bears witness; and their conflicting thoughts will accuse or perhaps excuse them on the day when, according to my gospel, God, through Jesus Christ, will judge the secret thoughts of all.

Gentiles do not have the Law in the way the Jews do, but Paul says that 'what the law requires is written on their hearts'. The NRSV's 'what the law requires' translates τὸ ἔργον τοῦ νόμου (lit. 'the work of the law'). This is an unusual expression found nowhere else in the NT or the LXX. Some scholars argue that this cannot be an allusion to the new covenant promise in Jeremiah 31:33 because Paul does not speak of 'the Law', but 'the work of the Law' written on Gentile hearts. [19] They argue that τὰ τοῦ νόμου must refer to something more limited and vague than the law understood in any comprehensive way.[20] However, Gathercole rightly points out that while the scope of the phrase *ta tou* is general in its NT usage it is also nearly always inclusive and comprehensive in meaning. Thus, for example, the contrast between 'the things of God' and 'the things of men' referred to in Matthew 16:23/Mark 8:33 (οὐ φρονεῖς τὰ τοῦ θεοῦ ἀλλὰ τὰ τῶν ἀνθρώπων) is comprehensive in meaning. Even when a contrast is not implied Paul uses such phrases in a comprehensive way (*cf.* Rom 14:19: 'Let us therefore make every effort to do what leads to peace [τὰ τῆς εἰρήνης] and to mutual edification'; 1 Cor 13:11: 'When I was a child, I talked like a child, I thought like a child, I reasoned like a child. When I became a man,

---

[19] Jeffrey S. Lamp, "Paul, the Law, Jews, and Gentiles: A Contextual and Exegetical Reading of Romans 2:12-16," *JETS* 42 (1999), 37-51, 47, argues against an allusion to Jer 31:33 on the grounds that Paul speaks of τὸ ἔργον τοῦ νόμου (the work of the law) being written on their hearts, not (ὁ) νόμος ([the] law) as in Jeremiah 31:33, but this appears to be a splitting of hairs. Mark D. Mathewson, "Moral intuitionism and the Law Inscribed on Our Hearts," *JETS* 42 (1999), 629-643, 633-642 also argues against an allusion to Jer 31:33, suggesting instead that Paul has in mind 'a moderate moral intuitionism', a 'natural ability of the mind to grasp immediately God's moral demands in an a priori manner'.

[20] So, *e.g.* James D. G. Dunn, *Romans* 1—8 (WBC 38b; Dallas, TX: Word, 1988), 105; Brendan Byrne, *Romans* (Sacra Pagina 6; Collegeville, MN: Liturgical Press, 1996), 105.

I put childish ways [τὰ τοῦ νηπίου] behind me'; 2 Cor 11:30: 'If I must boast, I will boast of the things that show my weakness [τὰ τῆς ἀσθενείας]'). There is, then, nothing to suggest that the meaning of τὰ τοῦ νόμου is anything but comprehensive here in Romans 2:14.[21] This leaves open the possibility that Paul is indeed speaking of Gentile Christians in Romans 2:14-15; Gentiles on whose hearts the law has been written in accordance with the promise of the new covenant in Jeremiah 31:33.[22] Paul certainly believed that the law is 'fulfilled' (though not observed in all its detail) by those who believe in Jesus Christ and walk in the Spirit (Rom 8:3-4; 13:10; Gal 5:13-25). Wright is correct when he says: 'I find it next to impossible that Paul could have written this phrase, with its overtones of Jeremiah's new covenant promise, simply to refer to pagans who happen by accident to share some of Israel's moral teaching. More likely by a million miles that he is hinting quietly, and proleptically, at what he will say far more fully later on: that Gentile Christians belong within the new covenant.'[23]. If it is an allusion to Jeremiah 31:33 then 'the law written on their hearts' means much more than an innate moral sense. It means a godly moral disposition. What is implied by Jeremiah 31:33 is expressed more fully by Ezekiel 36:26-27: 'I will give you a new heart and put a new spirit in you; I will remove from you your heart of stone and give you a heart of flesh. And I will put my Spirit in you and move you to follow my decrees and be careful to keep my laws.' If this is the case then we can say, in relation to the Law and the Spirit, Paul taught that with the coming of Christ and bestowal of the Spirit upon those who believe in him, what the law required of the Jews would be written upon the hearts of the Gentiles by the Spirit.[24]

---

[21] S. J. Gathercole, "A Law unto Themselves: The Gentiles in Romans 2.14-15 Revisited," *JSNT* 85 (2002), 27-49, 34.

[22] Akio Ito, "ΝΟΜΟΣ (ΤΩΝ) ἘΡΓΩΝ and ΝΟΜΟΣ ΠΙΣΤΕΩΣ. The Pauline Rhetoric and Theology of **ΝΟΜΟΣ**," *NovT* 45 (2003), 237-259, 250-251, and "Romans 2: A Deuteronomistic Reading," *JSNT* 59 (1995), 21-37, 28-35, reaches the same conclusion.

[23] N. T. Wright, "The Law in Romans 2," in *Paul and the Mosaic law* (ed. James D. G. Dunn; Grand Rapids: Eerdmans, 2001),131-150, 147. Wright adds: 'In short, if 2.25-9 is an anticipation of fuller statements, within the letter, of Paul's belief that Christian Gentiles do indeed fulfill the law even though they do not possess it, 2.13-14 looks as though it is a still earlier statement of very nearly the same point' (147).

[24] They would be like the 'true Jew' of Rom 2:28-29: 'For a person is not a Jew who is one outwardly, nor is true circumcision something external and physical. Rather, a person is a Jew who is one inwardly, and real circumcision is a matter of the heart—it is spiritual and not literal.' *Cf.* also Deut 30:6: 'Moreover, the LORD your God will circumcise your heart and the heart of your descendants, so that you will love the LORD your God with all your heart and with all your soul, in order that you may live.'

## The Law Fulfilled by Those who Live by the Spirit

Despite the fact that Paul strenuously argued that believers are no longer under the Mosaic law as the regulatory norm for their lives, in a number of passages he affirms that the law is fulfilled in the lives of those who live by the Spirit. One of the most important of these passages is Romans 8:2-4.

> For the law of the Spirit of life in Christ Jesus has set you free from the law of sin and of death. For God has done what the law, weakened by the flesh, could not do: by sending his own Son in the likeness of sinful flesh, and to deal with sin, he condemned sin in the flesh, so that the just requirement of the law might be fulfilled in us, who walk not according to the flesh but according to the Spirit.

The expressions, 'the law of the Spirit of life' and 'the law of sin and death', have both sometimes been interpreted as references to the Mosaic law,[25] and if this is the case they would provide us with important clues to Paul's understanding of the law and the Spirit. The two expressions would then reflect two aspects of the law. Dunn says:

> The law caught in the nexus of sin and death, where it is met only by σάρξ, is the law as γράμμα, caught in the old epoch, abused and destructive ... but the law rightly understood, and responded to ἐν πνεύματι οὐ γράμματι is pleasing to God (2:29). The twofold law of v. 2 therefore simply restates the two-sidedness of the law expounded in 7:7-25.[26]

One of the problems with this view is that it implies Romans 8:2 is saying that the law rightly understood sets us free from the law wrongly understood. But this is not what Paul has in mind. In the very next verse (Rom 8:3) he speaks of God sending his Son to deal with the problem of sin, something that the law (however understood) was unable to do. This, of course, was also in Paul's mind when he wrote Romans 7:7-25, except that there the law was not only unable to effect the deliverance, but as the unwilling ally of sin, was itself part of the problem. It is therefore better to interpret the expressions, 'the law of the Spirit of life' and 'the law of sin and death', as the liberating power of the Spirit and the dominion of sin respectively.[27] It was the power of sin (admittedly using the law as

---

[25] So e.g. Dunn, Romans 1-8, 416-419.

[26] Romans 1-8, 416-417.

[27] So most commentators, including more recently, Ziesler, Romans, 202; C. E. B. Cranfield, A Critical and Exegetical commentary on the Epistle to the Romans, vol.1 (ICC; Edinburgh:

an unwilling ally) that caused the 'I' of Romans 7:7-25 so much anguish. It is through (justification and) the reception of the Spirit that believers are delivered from sin's dominion.[28] The law of the Spirit and life and the law of sin and death understood in this way do not then contribute to our understanding of Paul's views concerning the relationship between the Mosaic law and the Spirit of God following the coming of Christ

In Romans 8:3a Paul speaks of 'what the law, weakened by the flesh, could not do',[29] without explaining what exactly that was. However, in Romans 8:3b-4 he proceeds to say that God has done what the law proved unable to do, that is, 'by sending his own Son in the likeness of sinful flesh,[30] and to deal with sin,[31] he condemned sin in the flesh[32] so that the just requirement of the law might be

---

T. & T. Clark, 1975), 364, 373-376; Douglas J. Moo, The Epistle to the Romans (NICNT; Grand Rapids: Eerdmans, 1996), 473-477. Cf. Heikki Räisänen, Paul and the Law (Philadelphia: Fortress, 1986), 50-52.

[28] This is not to say that in Romans Paul implies that believers no longer struggle with sin, but rather that this struggle does not have to end in the sort of defeat portrayed in 7:7-25. The new alternatives are expressed in 8:12-13: 'So then, brothers and sisters, we are debtors, not to the flesh, to live according to the flesh—for if you live according to the flesh, you will die; but if by the Spirit you put to death the deeds of the body [here obviously a synonym for flesh], you will live.'

[29] J. F. Bayes, "The Translation of Romans 8:3," *ExpTim* 111 (1999),14-16, 14 suggests the following translation of Rom 8:3: 'For this being the Law's disability *while it used to be weak in the sphere of the flesh*, God having sent his own Son in the likeness of sinful flesh and for sin, condemned sin in the flesh' (italics added). Bayes argues then that 'Romans 8:3a implies that there is another sphere, that which Paul denominates "the Spirit", where the law is weak no longer .... In the power of the Spirit the law has become a mighty instrument for the sanctification of the believer' (14). With some qualification this is true, the qualification being that the law is not reintroduced as a regulatory norm, but used as a witness to the gospel and, when read paradigmatically in the light of Christ, as providing guidelines for Christian living.

[30] There is ongoing debate whether Paul's 'in the likeness of sinful flesh' (ἐν ὁμοιώματι σαρκὸς ἁμαρτίας) implies a distinction or identification between Christ's humanity and ours. *Cf., e.g.* more recently, Vincent P. Branick, "The Sinful Flesh of the Son of God (Rom 8:3): A Key Image of Pauline Theology," *CBQ* 47 (1985), 246-262, 247-252; Florence Morgan Gillman, "Another Look at Romans 8:3: 'In the Likeness of Sinful Flesh'," *CBQ* 49 (1987), 597-604, 600-604.

[31] It is not necessary for our purposes to decide between the two possible interpretations of περὶ ἁμαρτίας here, whether it means 'as a sin offering' (following the LXX usage of περὶ ἁμαρτίας), or more generally 'to deal with sin'.

[32] Paul's expression, 'he condemned sin in the flesh' (κατέκρινεν τὴν ἁμαρτίαν ἐν τῇ σαρκί) is ambiguous. It could be taken to mean either 'God condemned the sin which is found in human flesh', or 'God condemned sin in the flesh of Christ'. The former is unlikely because, as Ziesler, *Romans*, 205, points out, 'sin in the flesh' is a tautology. There is no other sort of sin on the horizon in this context. The latter is preferable as it makes sense to speak of God condemning sin in the flesh (of Christ), another way of saying that in the purpose of God, Christ in his death became a curse for us, bearing the burden and penalty of our sins (*cf.* Gal 3:13). Ziesler, surprisingly interprets the verse to mean that 'Christ, when in the flesh,

fulfilled in us who walk not according to the flesh but according to the Spirit'. What the law cannot do, Paul implies, is to bring about the fulfilment of its own just requirement in the lives of those who lived under it.[33] The just requirement of the law has sometimes been interpreted to mean 'all that the law requires'. Such an approach has obvious problems because Paul clearly did not expect believers to fulfil all the demands of the law (circumcision, one of the basic demands of the law, Paul argued, was definitely not required of Gentile believers). A further difficulty for this view, often overlooked, is that Paul refers to the 'just requirement' (singular-- δικαίωμα), not the 'just requirements' (plural-- δικαιώματα), and while the plural, δικαιώματα, is used in the NT and the LXX to refer to the sum of the law's demands, the singular, δικαίωμα is not.[34]

Ziesler, taking note of the singular δικαίωμα, suggests that when Paul speaks of the just requirement of the law in Romans 8:4 he means the tenth commandment, which he had in mind throughout Romans 7:7-25. Because, on this view, Romans 8:4 refers only to the command not to covet, it cannot be taken to refer to the sum of the law's demands (nor the love command, nor the moral law).[35] While is important to note Paul's use of the singular form δικαίωμα in Romans 8:4, it is not at all certain that it should be interpreted as narrowly as Ziesler suggests. Even interpreting it in the light of the Paul's reference to the tenth commandment in Romans 7:7-25, we need to remember that there Paul used the tenth commandment as a paradigm for the whole law, as Ziesler himself acknowledges.[36]

A good case can be made for interpreting 'the just requirement of the law' as the love commandment (despite Ziesler's dismissal of this view), especially in the light of the parallels between Romans 8:4 and Galatians 5:13-16. It is precisely at these points in Romans and Galatians respectively that (i) the notion of the Spirit first

---

condemned sin, either by his sinless life or by his death', failing it seems to recognize that God, not Christ, is the subject of the sentence.

[33] It is important to note that the law was unable to do this, not because of any imperfection in itself, but because its power to do so was weakened by the flesh. This is what Paul argues at length in Rom 7:7-25. That Paul speaks about the law's inability to bring about the fulfilment of its own righteous demand because of the weakness of the flesh excludes (*contra* Morrison and Woodhouse, "The Coherence of Romans 7:1-8:8," 15) any interpretation of 'the just requirement of the law' as death.

[34] *Cf.* J. A. Ziesler, "The Just Requirement of the Law (Romans 8.4)," *AusBR* 35 (1987), 77-82, 78.

[35] Ziesler, "The Just Requirement of the Law," 80.

[36] Ziesler, "The Just Requirement of the Law," 80.

comes to the fore, (ii) the Spirit/flesh antithesis is mentioned for the first time, and (iii) there is a striking convergence of the concepts of freedom, fulfilment, walking in the Spirit and the negative aspects of the flesh.[37] In the light of the striking similarities between Romans 8:4 and Galatians 5:13-16, it would seem to be desirable to interpret the former in the light of the latter, and to say that the fulfilment of the just requirement of the law (in Rom 8:4) is best understood in terms of the love of neighbour (in Gal 5:13-16).[38]

It is significant that this text speaks about 'the just requirement of the law' *being fulfilled* (divine passive) in those who walk according to the Spirit, not about believers *fulfilling* (active) this requirement. The fulfilment of the law in believers is therefore not achieved because they are continuously careful to observe its many stipulations. Rather it is fulfilled in them as they walk according to the Spirit and as by the Spirit they put to death the deeds of the flesh (Rom 8:13). Thus the real contrast between the law and the Spirit in Romans 8:3-4 is that while the requirement of the law is just, the law was powerless to bring about the fulfilment of that just requirement in sinful human beings. However, God brings about this fulfilment in the lives of those who walk according to the Spirit.

A second passage in which Paul affirms that the law is fulfilled in the lives of those who live by the Spirit is Romans 13:8-10. Here the apostle exhorts his readers, as part of their grateful response for the mercies of God, to:

> Owe no one anything, except to love one another; for the one who loves another has fulfilled the law. The commandments, 'You shall not commit adultery; You shall not murder; You shall not steal; You shall not covet'; and any other commandment, are summed up in this word, 'Love your neighbour as yourself'. Love does no wrong to a neighbour; therefore, love is the fulfilling of the law.

Paul's intention is to exhort his readers to love one another and the idea that love is the fulfilment of the law is brought in to bolster that

---

[37] *Cf.* Richard W. Thompson, "How is the Law fulfilled in Us? An Interpretation of Rom 8:4," *LS* 11 (1986), 31-41, 32-33, who cites the observations of H. W. M. van de Sandt, "Research into Rom. 8:4a: The Legal Claim of the Law." *Bijdragen* 37 (1976), 252-269.

[38] Such a conclusion is strengthened by the fact that, in Romans 13:8-10, Paul says all the other commandments are summed up in the commandment, Love your neighbour as yourself, and concludes: 'therefore, love is the fulfilling of the law' (see discussion below), *contra* Wright, *The Climax of the Covenant*, 211-212, who rejects this view, arguing instead that τὸ δικαίωμα τοῦ νόμου means 'the just decree of the law', *i.e.* 'the decree that gives life in accordance with the covenant'.

exhortation.[39] It is important to note that Paul is not saying that love will lead believers to carry out all that the law demands (which would have to include, *e.g.* the practice of circumcision, obedience to calendrical rules, and the observance of food taboos; things which Paul clearly thought were not obligatory for believers, *cf.* Rom 2:26; 14:2-6). What he says is that love *fulfils* the law, and that is clearly something different. When Paul claims that love is the fulfilment of the law, he has in mind particularly those laws that relate to the neighbour's wellbeing. Thus he cites four commandments from the second table of the Decalogue (only the commandment not to bear false witness is omitted from Paul's list), and says that these 'and any other commandment, are summed up in this word, "Love your neighbour as yourself"' (Rom 13:9). It is clear that what Paul is asserting here is of limited application: love is the fulfilment of the law in so far as the law is concerned to ensure no harm is done to one's neighbour (Rom 13:10); he is not saying that love leads believers to observe all the demands of the Mosaic law. This text has important implications for our understanding of the relationship of the law and the Spirit in Paul's gospel. His gospel is not antinomian, for it results in a fulfilment of the law. However, this does not mean a reinstatement of the law. Rather, the effect of Paul's gospel is that believers, by walking in the Spirit, are enabled to love one another, so that what the law sought, but was unable to produce, is fulfilled in them.

A third passage, Galatians 5:14-18, makes a similar point:

> For the whole law is summed up in a single commandment, 'You shall love your neighbour as yourself.' If, however, you bite and devour one another, take care that you are not consumed by one another. Live by the Spirit, I say, and do not gratify the desires of the flesh. For what the flesh desires is opposed to the Spirit, and what the Spirit desires is opposed to the flesh; for these are opposed to each other, to prevent you from doing what you want. But if you are led by the Spirit, you are not subject to the law.

Here obedience to the love command is seen as fulfilment of the *whole* law, but this does not mean carrying out all the law's demands (in Galatians Paul argues strenuously against the need for Gentiles to be circumcised). Once again Paul has in mind the way

---

[39] Oda Wischmeyer, "Das Gebot der Nächstenliebe bei Paulus. Eine traditionsgeschichtliche Untersuchung," *BZ* 30 (1986), 161-187, 182, goes too far when he says that Rom 13:8-10 was part of Paul's program of abolishing the law by means of the law.

believers relate to one another.[40] And the ability to fulfil the law in this way is linked to living 'by the Spirit', and this is linked in turn to freedom from the law: 'if you are led by the Spirit, you are not subject to the law'. Paul is here implying what he clearly asserted in Romans 7:6, *i.e.* believers' release from the law enables them to live 'the new life of the Spirit'.

A fourth passage, Galatians 5:22-23, is also significant. Having listed the 'works of the flesh', Paul then lists the 'fruit of the Spirit': 'By contrast, the fruit of the Spirit is love, joy, peace, patience, kindness, generosity, faithfulness, gentleness, and self-control. There is no law against such things.'[41] The first element of the fruit of the Spirit is love. Against this there is no law, and in fact, as the apostle says love is the fulfilment of the law. As far as the relationship between the law and the Spirit is concerned, then, the Spirit is the one who enables believers to fulfil the law, doing this by overcoming the desires of the flesh and producing the fruit of love in their lives.

## Conclusion

On first reading of Paul's letters to the Galatians and the Romans especially, one could get the impression that Paul's attitude to the Mosaic law was largely negative, and that with the coming of the Spirit following the death and resurrection of Christ there was no further place for the law in the lives of believers. However, the material surveyed in this article reveals that Paul's teaching about the law and the Spirit is more complex than that. Our findings can be summarised as follows.

In what Paul says in 2 Corinthians 3:7-11 concerning ministry under the old and new covenants a stark contrast is implied between the role of the law and the Spirit. The law condemns and kills,

---

[40] Stephen Westerholm has shown that in the three places where Paul speaks about believers fulfilling the law (Rom 8:4; 13:8-10; Gal 5:14), he is *describing* not prescribing Christian behaviour. Paul's prescriptive statements are based on the new life in the Spirit that those in Christ enjoy. His references to fulfilling the law in these contexts are made to describe the results of new life in the Spirit. He is not re-introducing the law as a regulatory norm for those who are in Christ. See *Israel's Law and the Church's Faith: Paul and his Recent Interpreters* (Grand Rapids: Eerdmans, 1988), 201-205, where Westerholm summarizes his article, "On Fulfilling the Whole Law (Gal 5:14)", *SEÅ* 51-52 (1986-1987), 229-237.

[41] R. A. Campbell, '"Against such things there is no Law"? Galatians 5:23b again', *ExpTim* 107 (1996), 271-272, says that τῶν τοιούτων in Gal 5:23 should be translated 'such people', not 'such things'. Then the parenthetical remark in 5:23 ('there is no condemnation for people like that') would balance the earlier statement in 5:21 ('those who do such things will not inherit the kingdom of God').

whereas the Spirit gives life. In Galatians 3:13-14 and 4:4-6 the apostle argues that the Jewish people had to be redeemed from the curse of the law (it condemned and killed) so that they might receive the promised Holy Spirit, and so that in turn the promise might extend to and the Spirit be received by the Gentiles as well. In Galatians 3:1-5 Paul indicates that the reception of the Spirit by the Gentiles and their ongoing experience of the Spirit was independent of their observance of the law, and in Romans 7:4-6 and Galatians 5:16-18 he even teaches that it is necessary to be freed from the demands of the law in order to 'bear fruit for God'. And yet, paradoxically, the Spirit writes the law upon the hearts of the Gentiles (Rom 2:14-16), and the law is 'fulfilled' in the lives of those who walk by the Spirit (Rom 8:3-4; 13:8-10; Gal 5:14-18, 22-23), though this does not mean they carry out all the demands of the law, but by walking in the way of love what the law was meant to achieve is produced in their lives by the Spirit.

As a final comment it may be added that, whereas the demands of the Mosaic law are no longer the regulatory norm for believers, the Old Testament is nevertheless their Scripture that when illuminated by the Spirit is seen to be a witness to Christ and a source of instruction for godly living when read paradigmatically in the light of the gospel (*cf.* 2 Tim 3:16-17).

# The Theological Interpretation of Scripture with Special Attention to the Pioneering Insights of Athanasius and Augustine

## Kevin Giles

Independent Scholar, Melbourne

Abstract

*The essay examines the processes employed by two of the outstanding post-Nicene fathers, Athanasius and Augustine, in order to provide an assessment of what a "theological interpretation of Scripture" entails. The paper concludes that the theological interpretation of Scripture involves an approach to the Bible that takes proper account of its unity in diversity, duly recognises the history of interpretation, and is aware of both the role and limitations of analogy and metaphor.*

I have been active in the theological enterprise for more than forty years but only in recent times have come to some convictions in my own mind as to what the theological interpretation of Scripture entails. In these forty years I have often heard the expression, and in the last ten years I have read a number of books that have the stated aim of explaining what this is. I have learnt something from most of them but found none of them completely satisfying. It was only when I began to study the biblical basis for the doctrine of the Trinity and its developing historical articulation that I came to certain personal conclusions as to what the theological interpretation of scripture involves.

## My introduction to the historical and critical study of scripture

I arrived at Moore Theological College, Sydney, in 1964 as a naïve and enthusiastic young convert who was determined to work hard at his studies. These were the early days of post Second World War evangelical scholarship. We were encouraged to be scholarly but frequently warned of 'critical scholarship,' which was identified with liberal scholarship. Nevertheless, while avoiding the term 'critical' we were thoroughly grounded in the critical and historical study of the scriptures.¹ We were taught that our goal in studying the Bible was to work out what the words on the page would have meant to the author and his readers. The historical meaning of every text was our goal. A knowledge of the original languages was essential for this task, as was a good knowledge of the various historical and cultural contexts in which each book was originally composed. In addition, we were introduced to textual criticism, form criticism, source criticism and in the last year of my four year course, Don Robinson introduced us to the new redaction criticism. Later, in my post graduate studies at Durham University England, I completed a thesis on the church in the theology of St Luke predicated on redaction criticism. Later, as I continued reading, I learnt about narrative criticism, sociological criticism and rhetorical criticism.

With this firm grounding in the critical and historical study of scripture, I was supremely confident that I could work out what the scriptures taught on any matter. I was a competent in the science of biblical interpretation. What is more, I had come to internalise what my most formative teacher, Dr Broughton Knox, repeatedly claimed, 'everything I believe comes directly from the scriptures.' It became my conviction too that the Bible *alone* gave content to my beliefs and doctrines.

What unsettled my initial confidence that with the Bible in hand I could work out what the Bible taught on any matter and there could be little dispute, was when I got involved in the new debate on what the Bible taught on the status and ministry of women.² From the very beginning I saw clearly that one's answer almost entirely rested on the interpretation given to one text in the Bible, 1Timothy 2:11-14. If this text was interpreted to say that women should not exercise authority, especially as teachers in church, because God in creation had made woman 'second' and she was more prone to be 'deceived' than men, then women were the subordinated sex by God's decree. If on the other hand, the conclusion was reached that this text in fact was forbidding women who had been 'deceived' from teaching with unauthorised authority, as many believe the

---

¹ Of course rejecting completely naturalistic presuppositions.

² My first book on this topic was, *Women and Their Ministry: A case for equal ministries in the church today* (Melbourne: Dove Communications, 1977). I continue to publish on the status and ministry of women.

exceptional Greek word αὐθεντεῖν (*authentein*) implies,[3] and nothing in the creation stories subordinates women to men, then the substantial equality of the sexes could be taken as the God-given ideal. The question that this debate raised was, how determinative could one text be in the construction of any doctrine?

Later, I had another experience that made me question my conviction that everything I believed sprang immediately from the text of scripture. In writing a brief account of basic Christian doctrines, *Understanding the Christian Faith*,[4] I found that the Bible did not spell out the doctrines I was enunciating as clearly or unambiguously as I had anticipated. On every doctrine I studied I found texts that were in tension with what the agreed doctrine affirmed and thus to ground a doctrine in scripture I had to be selective, often explaining away texts that seemed to say the opposite of what the doctrine as received taught. For example, in discussing the doctrine of justification by grace alone, I had to explain why James insistence that we are saved by works was to be ignored. And in discussing the doctrine of the Trinity, why Jesus' words in John 14:28, 'the Father is greater than I' do not refer to the eternal relations between the Father and the Son. I lived with these questions in my mind for many years still confident that all that the evangelical scholar needed for 'doing' theology was good interpretative skills. I still voiced from time to time my mantra, 'Everything I believe comes directly from the Bible.'

Only gradually did I come to recognise that while the critical and historical exegesis of scripture was the best way to discover the historical meaning of individual texts, it also tended to highlight the diversity in Scripture, thus complicating the theological endeavour. As I was discovering this so too were other evangelicals. Thus in the last twenty years or so numerous studies on what is involved in 'doing' evangelical theology have been written, [5] many of which

---

[3] See the full discussion of the meaning of this word in P. B. Payne, *Man and woman in Christ* (Zondervan, Grand Rapids, 2009), 361-398.

[4] (Canberra: Acorn, 1982).

[5] For example, A. McGrath, *Genesis of Doctrine* (Oxford: Basil Blackwell, 1990); J. G. Stackhouse, ed., *Evangelical Futures: A Conversation on Theological Method* (Grand Rapids, Baker, 2000); R. Lints, *The Fabric of Theology: A Prolegomena to Evangelical Theology* (Grand Rapids: Eerdmans, 1993); S. J. Grenz, *Revisioning Evangelical Theology: A Fresh Agenda for the 21st Century* (Downers Grove, Ill.: InterVarsity, 1993); S. J. Grenz and J. H. Franke, *Beyond Foundationalism: Shaping Theology in a Postmodern Context* (Louisville: Westminster John Knox, 2001); J. S. Franke, *The Character of Theology: An Introduction to its Nature, Task and Purpose* (Grand Rapids, Baker, 2005); T. Griggs, *New Perspectives for Evangelical Theology: Engaging with God, Scripture and the World* (London: Routledge, 2010).

acknowledge that critical and historical exegesis needs to be complemented and supplemented by what is called 'the theological interpretation' of scripture.

Kevin Vanhoozer says, 'it is much easier to say what theological interpretation of the Bible is *not* rather than what it is.'[6] I agree. I have read widely on this topic and not been entirely satisfied by the answers given.[7] My own conclusion, which I have arrived at by reading the church fathers, the Reformers and the great Dutch theologians of the nineteenth and twentieth centuries,[8] as well as contemporary discussions on this matter, is that the theological interpretation of scripture is characterised by four things. It assumes that the Bible is to be read:

Canonically, on the premise that the overall teaching of scripture must determine and inform the meaning of individual and isolated texts.

The Old Testament is to be read in the light of the New Testament.

1. The historical meaning of a biblical text does not necessarily exhaust the meaning of a text.[9]

2. The best guide to a right interpretation of the scriptures in relation to any historically developed doctrine is the theological tradition; what the best of theologians across the centuries have concluded the scriptures teach.

To justify these conclusions I turn to Athanasius and Augustine who pioneered this way of appropriating scripture in the theological

---

[6] 'What is Theological Interpretation?' in Vanhoozer, *The Dictionary,* 19.

[7] For evangelical introductions to this subject see D. J. Treier, *Introducing Theological Interpretation of Scripture: Recovering a Christian Practice* (Grand Rapids, Mich. Baker, 2008), S. E. Fowl, *Theological Interpretation of Scripture* (Eugene, Or.: Cascade, 2009), K. J. Vanhoozer, 'What is Theological Interpretation of the Bible?' in, in Kevin J. Vanhoozer, *Dictionary for the Theological Interpretation of the Bible* (Grand Rapids, Mich.: Baker Academic, 2005); J. B. Green, *Practicing Theological Interpretation* (Grand Rapids: Baker, 2011), J. T. Billings, *The Word of God for the People of God: an entry to the theological interpretation of scripture* (Grand Rapids: Eerdmans, 2010).

[8] Such as A. Kuyper, H. Bavinck, L. Berkhof, and C. Berkouwer.

[9] Some scholars speak of the 'sensus plenior' of scripture, a Latin term for the idea that some texts may have a meaning not intended by the author but intended by God. Evangelicals often get concerned about this idea but there can be no questioning that the New Testament authors often take Old Testament texts that referred to Yahweh and apply them to Christ and that they often see a non-historical meaning and application of many Old Testament narratives (Cf. 1 Cor. 10:1-13, Gal. 4:21-31, Heb. 3:7-18 etc.).

quest, illustrating for us what is involved in 'the theological interpretation of scripture.'

## My change of mind

What helped me most of all in my quest to understand what was involved in 'doing' evangelical theology was my study of the doctrine of the Trinity. This has extended over a ten year period, with my first of three books on the Trinity published in 2002.[10] My historic mentors who forced me to rethink my position were first and foremost Athanasius and then Augustine. They had a very different way of 'doing' theology than I had taken on board as a contemporary evangelical. Athanasius' response to Arius left me breathtaken in its profundity and insight. He opened up a new world for me.

For Arius, and those who Athanasius calls 'the Arians,' their basic premise was that God is one, a Monad, and so the Son and the Spirit cannot be God in the same absolute sense as the Father. For them, the Son was created in time and as such is other in divine being and power than the Father. One text, Proverbs 8:22, 'The lord created (κτίζω) me at the beginning of his works' was for them conclusive evidence that they were right in arguing that the Son was created in time and thus other than the creator God in being and power. This was their knock down 'proof text' that they quoted *ad infinitum*. Then they found many other texts that seemed to support their view that Christ the Son of God was God in second degree. They noted passages that spoke of him as being sent by the Father, praying to the Father, doing the will of the Father, obeying the Father and confessing his ignorance of some things. And they made much of the fact that Jesus is called 'Son.' They argued sons are always set under their father. What we learn from this is that despite the fact that Arius' view of God was more Greek than Hebraic his case was entirely biblical. He appealed primarily to scripture and at least one verse seemed to say explicitly what he taught. The Son was created in time, and thus a creature, even if a creature greater than all other creatures.

---

[10] K. N. Giles, *The Trinity and Subordinationism: The Doctrine of God and the Contemporary Gender Debate* (Downers Grove, Ill., Intervarsity, 2002); *Jesus and the Father: Modern Evangelicals Reinvent the Doctrine of the Trinity* (Grand Rapids, Zondervan, 2006); *The Eternal Generation of the Son: Maintaining Orthodoxy in Trinitarian Theology* (Downers Grove, Ill., Intervarsity, 2012).

If Arius' creaturely understanding of Jesus Christ predicated, he believed, entirely on the Bible was to be defeated, some very deep theological thinking would be demanded. In this critical hour for the Christian faith God raised up two of the best theologians the world has known; Alexander bishop of Alexandria (d. 328) and Athanasius his successor (296-373). Alexander, Athanasius' theological mentor, seems to have foreshadowed most of the conclusions Athanasius reached but it was Athanasius that developed and promulgated them. He was a formidable theologian. His intellect was razor sharp, his grasp of scripture unequalled, his tenacity unremitting, and his tolerance of error minimal. In all his theological writings soteriology is always his central and primary concern. He argued consistently that only a perfectly adequate redemption could be achieved by a perfectly adequate redeemer. To fulfil this requirement Christ had to be at one and the same time fully God and fully man in the one person.

Athanasius was convinced first of all that Arius could not be right because his ideas were contrary to what 'the bishops who preceded us and our first catechising' had taught us regarding what scripture taught. His teaching was in opposition to 'the tradition of the fathers;'[11] what had been received 'from our fathers,'[12] that is, the teaching of the catholic theologians who had come before him. After the council of Nicea in 325, this 'tradition' was summed up in creed of Nicea with the added term *homoousios* (ὁμοούσιος), the Father and the Son are *one in being*. In his work, the *Defence of the Nicene Definition*, he gives a list of those before him who have concluded that the Scriptures teach that the Father and the Son are one in being.[13] It is this theological and exegetical tradition, what the fathers had agreed is the teaching of scripture overall, that was determinative for him in judging who was interpreting scripture correctly. Weinandy says,

> Athanasius opposed Arius, and those who later held similar positions, precisely because he was convinced that they interested

---

[11] *Council of Nicea*, 1.2 and note 3 (p. 75) in P. Schaff and H. Wace, eds, *The Nicene and Post Nicene Fathers*, 4, (New York: The Christian Literature Company, 1892), henceforth abbreviated as *NPNF*. In quoting Athanasius and Augustine I also give the page numbers from the designated translations as the references can be hard to find.

[12] *NPNF*, 4, *Discourses Against the Arians*, 1.3.8 (p. 310)

[13] *NPNF*, 4, *Nicene Definition*, 6.25-27 (pp. 166-169).

scripture apart from the ecclesial tradition. Theirs was a private and personal, and thus idiosyncratic, interpretation of scripture."[14]

In arguing this way Athanasius saw clearly that in coming to scripture to study any doctrine, what other godly and skilled exegetes had determined was the overall teaching of scripture on the matter under consideration was the best place to begin. Athanasius' appeal to 'the tradition of the fathers,' was not an appeal to a body of teaching separate to scripture but to how others he highly respected before him had interpreted Scripture. For him this kind of tradition prescribing how to rightly read scripture was authoritative. This he contrasted with 'the traditions of men,'[15] teaching without **scriptural support or worse, contrary to scripture, which he denigrated.**

Second, Athanasius recognised that in coming to scripture in any dispute where the biblical text says different or even seemingly contradictory things, a way of reading scripture – that is a hermeneutic - that resulted in harmony and consistency needed to be formulated. To grasp the true meaning of any individual text, he argued, the whole 'scope' (σκοπός) of scripture had to be kept in view. In regard to the Son of God he says, 'The scope and character of Holy Scripture... is this: it contains a double account of the Saviour; that he was ever God and is the Son, being the Father's Logos and Radiance and Wisdom; and that afterwards for us he took the flesh of a virgin... This scope is to be found throughout inspired Scripture.'[16] This 'double account' of the Saviour, he argued, is most clearly enunciated in John chapter 1, and Philippians 2:5-11. In his prologue to his Gospel, John juxtaposes the statements, "the word was God" (Jn 1:1), and 'the Word became flesh' (Jn 1:14) and in writing to the Philippians Paul says, Christ 'was equal with God but emptied himself, taking the form of a servant, being found in the likeness of men.'[17] Once this 'double account' is recognised, Athanasius argued, the scriptures can be seen to be giving consistent teaching. The texts that speak of the Son in all might, majesty and power speak of him as God. The texts that speak of him as praying to the Father, doing the will of the Father, obeying the Father and as ignorant of some things speak of

---

[14] Athanasius: *A Theological Introduction* (Hampshire England: Ashgate, 2007), 135.

[15] *NPNF*, 4, *Letter 2, Easter 330*, 5 (p. 511and following).

[16] *NPNF*, 4, *Discourses*, 3.26.26-29 (p. 409).

[17] *NPNF*, 4, *Discourses*, 3.27.29 (p. 409).

him as God in the 'form of a servant,' in his earthly ministry for our salvation. For Athanasius, the Son is God eternally one in being and power with the Father, and in his incarnate ministry in the economy of salvation he is temporally subordinate to the Father by reason of him taking on human flesh.

With these two principles established Athanasius was ready to address the Arian proof text, Proverbs 8:22. He gives more space to refuting the Arian understanding of Proverbs 8:22 than any other of the numerous texts they quoted – 36 pages in the Schaff and Wace translation of his Discourses Against the Arians, in The Nicene and Post-Nicene Fathers.[18] His major objection to the Arian interpretation of this one text is that in the light of the whole 'scope' of scripture it cannot be correct. For him, it was clear the Bible as a whole teaches that the Son is not a creature, created in time. He is the eternal Son, ever with the Father, his very image; he is 'the proper offspring' of the Father, 'in all things like him;' 'he and the Father work as one;' 'he who has seen him has seen the Father.'[19]

Then as supporting arguments, more briefly put, he argues that,

1. The Arian proof text, Proverbs 8:22, is from the book of Proverbs and thus what is said 'is not said plainly, but is put forth latently,' the sense being 'hidden.'[20]

2. What is said in Proverbs 8:22 is 'not signifying the essence of his [the Son's] Godhead, nor his own everlasting and genuine generation from the Father ... but his manhood and economy towards us.'[21] In other words, the text speaks of the creation of the man Jesus of Nazareth in time and space. And,

3. the *eternal begetting* of the Son is spoken of in Proverbs 8:25, 'Before the mountains, and before the earth, and before the waters, and before all the hills, he begets me.'[22] This text, he holds, makes it plain that the Son is not 'a creature by

---

[18] *NPNF*, 4, *Discourses*, 2.16.18 to 2.22.82 (pp 357-393).

[19] These arguments are reiterated time and time again in *NPNF*, 4, *Discourses*, 2.16.18 to 2.22.82 (pp. 357-393).

[20] *NPNF*, 4, *Discourses*, 2.19.44 (p. 372).

[21] *NPNF*, 4, *Discourses*, 2.19.45 (p. 372). See also 2.20.51 (p. 376), 2.20.55, 56 (p. 378).

[22] *NPNF*, 4, *Discourses*, 2.22.80 (p. 392).

nature and essence, but as he himself [God the Father] had added an offspring.'²³

In seeking to clarify the issues, Athanasius sharply distinguishes the words, 'begotten' (γεννητός) and 'created' (γένετος).²⁴ He endorses speaking of the Son as 'begotten' (γεννάω) or as the Father's 'offspring' (γέννημα), first of all because he believes this is how the Bible speaks of the Son, and second, because for him these words speak of a father-son relationship. He says, they 'signify a Son, and beholding the Son we see the Father.'²⁵ Sons for him are of the same being or nature as their father.

Athanasius' exegesis of the Greek of Proverbs 8:22 would not pass the scrutiny of an evangelical who insists that the critical and historical meaning of any text is determinative. They would note that the New Testament definitely identifies Jesus Christ with divine Wisdom (1 Cor. 1:24, etc.) and the Proverbs text speaks of the creation of Wisdom in time. Nevertheless, Athanasius' conclusion must be right. The Bible read holistically excludes the idea that Jesus the Son of God is a creature. And today we are sure he was right because for all contemporary evangelicals the Hebrew text is authoritative scripture. In the Hebrew, the word in contention is קנני, best translated as "brought me forth."²⁶ It does not speak of a creative act in time.

Athanasius finds positive textual support for his conviction that an 'eternal begetting' of the Son is the best way to explain the Father-Son relationship in Old Testament texts which speak of God begetting a Son or divine Wisdom, texts 'the fathers' before him had quoted: Proverbs 8:25,²⁷ Psalms 2:7,²⁸ 45:1, ²⁹110:3,³⁰ and Isaiah

---

²³ *NPNF*, 4, *Discourses*, 2.22.80 (p. 392).

²⁴ On these words see R. P. C. Hanson, The Search for the Christian Doctrine of God (Edinburgh: T&T Clark, 1988), 203-204, and, P. Christou, 'Uncreated and Created, Unbegotten and Begotten in the Theology of Athanasius of Alexandria,' *Augustinianum*, 12/3 (1973), pp. 399-409.

²⁵ *NPNF*, 4, *Discourses*, 1.5.16 (p. 316).

²⁶ Bruce Vawter, 'Prov. 8:22: Wisdom and Creation,' *Journal of Biblical Literature*, 9 (1980), pp. 205-16.

²⁷ *NPNF*, 4, *Statement of Faith*, (p. 85), *Defence of the Nicene Definition*, 13 (p. 158), 26 (p. 168), *Discourses*, 2.17.32 (p. 365), 4.23 (p. 442).

²⁸ *NPNF*, 4, *Defence of the Nicene Definition*, 13 (p. 158), *Discourses*, 2.16.23 (p. 360), 2.21.57 (p. 379), 4.24 (p. 442), etc.

²⁹ *NPNF*, 4, *Disposition of Arius*, 3 9 (p. 70), *Defence of the Nicene Definition*, 13, (p. 158), 21 (p. 164), *Discourses*, 4.24 (p. 442) etc.

53:8.³¹ His primary appeal was to the Old Testament, but for him as with all the other church fathers this was Christian scripture just as much as the New Testament. He did not think for a moment that the meaning of any Old Testament text was limited to its historical meaning. What is more he concluded, going beyond what these texts actually said, that if any of these texts spoke in their historical context of an human begetting in time, when applied to the Son of God who is God they spoke of an eternal begetting. For Athanasius, the human is temporal, the divine is eternal.

Another very significant insight Athanasius made in regard to rightly interpreting scripture in the theological enterprise was that human words such as 'father, 'son,' and 'begetting' used of the divine persons in the scriptures could not be understood literally, that is in a creaturely sense. He would thus not allow that the begetting of the Son was to be likened to human begetting, a temporal creative act, or that because Jesus is named 'the Son' he was like human son set under his father. For Athanasius, defining or fully understanding divine relations or divine origination in terms of human relations or human origination is not possible.³² He does not use the words 'analogical' or 'metaphorical' to describe human language used of God but he clearly recognizes and says that that human language used of God should not be taken literally, or to use the technical term, 'univocally.' He writes,

> For God creates and to create is also ascribed to men; and God has being, and men are said to have received from God this gift also. Yet does God create as men do? Or is his being as man's being? Perish the thought; we understand the terms in one sense of God, and in another of men. ³³

And,

> For in this again the generation of the Son exceeds and transcends the thoughts of man, that we become father of our own children in time, since we ourselves first were not and then came into being; but God, in that he is ever is, is ever Father of the Son.³⁴

---

[30] *NPNF*, 4, *Disposition*, 3 (p. 70), *Defence of the Nicene Definition*, 23 (p. 164), *Discourses*, 2.21.57 (p. 379), 4.24 (p. 442), etc.

[31] *NPNF*, 4, *Statement of Faith*, 1 (p. 84), *Councils of Ariminum and Seleucia*, 27 (p. 466) - in this case, quoting others.

[32] See in particular, *NPNF*, 4, *Nicene Definition*, 3.11 (p. 157).

[33] *NPNF*, 4, *Nicene Definition*, 3.11 (p. 157).

[34] *NPNF*, 4, *Nicene Definition*, 3.12 (p. 157).

And,

> If God be not as a man, as he is not, we must not impute to him the attributes of man."[35]

Long before Aquinas came to discuss the nature of human language Athanasius recognised that all human language used of God is 'analogical,' even if he did not use this term.

### Augustine

Like Athanasius, Augustine comes to scripture in his study on the Trinity presupposing that what the great catholic theologians prior to him had taught on the Trinity is correct, and as such the key to a right reading of scripture. He says,

> The purpose of all the catholic commentators I have been able to read on the divine books of both testaments, who have written before me on the Trinity which God is, has been to teach that according to the scriptures, Son and Holy Spirit in the inseparable equality of one substance present a divine unity; and **therefore there are not three Gods but one. ..."**.[36]

Given this premise, Augustine's sees his task as not trying to prove from scripture the doctrine of the Trinity but to show that the received doctrine makes the most sense of, and reflects most accurately, what the scriptures teach as a whole. He is very aware that he needs sure guidance on how to rightly interpret scripture because 'the heretics try to defend their false and misleading opinions from these very scriptures.'[37] And because in scripture there are seeming 'contradictions'[38] and 'multifarious diversity.'[39]

In reply to the heretics who quote isolated texts that they think make the Son "less than" the Father he argues that the catholic theologian concentrates on 'utterances of the clearest and most consistent testimonies'[40] that unambiguously affirm that the Son and the Holy Spirit are God without any caveats.[41] He cannot allow

---

[35] *NPNF*, 4, *Discourses*,1.6.21 (p. 319)

[36] *The Trinity: Introduction, Translation and Notes*, E. Hill ed. (New York: New City, 1991), 1. 2.7 (p. 69). All references from *De Trinitate* are taken from this translation.

[37] *The Trinity*, 1.1.6 (p. 69).

[38] *The Trinity*, 1.4.22 (p. 82).

[39] *The Trinity*, 2, prologue 1 (p. 97).

[40] *The Trinity,* 1.1.9 (p. 71)

[41] *The Trinity*, 1.1. 9-13 (pp. 70-73).

that texts such a John 14:28, 'the Father is greater than I,' Proverbs 8:22, 'the Lord created me,' or 1 Corinthians 15:28, 'then the Son himself will also be made subject' that the 'heretics' love to quote can determine doctrine. For him the big picture, what he calls, 'the whole range of scriptures,'[42] is determinative and discordant texts must be interpreted in this light.

Returning to the matter of how to rightly appeal to scripture in the theological enterprise, early in book 2 of *De Trinitate*, Augustine lays down two, what he calls 'canonical rules,'[43] for reading scripture faithfully. He argues these are implied in scripture and prescribed by 'learned catholic expositors.'[44] The first and most important of these 'rules' is that all texts that speak of Christ as equal in divinity, majesty and authority with the Father refer to him 'in the form of God,' and all texts that speak of his human limitations, subordination and obedience refer exclusively to him in 'the form of a servant,' as the incarnate Son.[45] This hermeneutical rule, as we would call it, he found spelt out in Philippians 2:4-11, a text to which he repeatedly returns. The second rule he gives is that texts that speak of the Son doing the Father's will, or judging on behalf of the Father, or of his 'begetting' and 'sending,' 'mark him neither as less nor equal, but only intimate that he is from the Father.'[46] A third rule appears right at the commencement of *De Trinitate*. Augustine gives it as a premise that the God of the Bible should not be defined 'in bodily terms.'[47] Like Athanasius, Augustine sees clearly that biblical language is, to use later terms, analogical and metaphorical. Creaturely words such as 'father,' 'son,' and 'sending' when applied to God are not to be understood in a creaturely sense, that is univocally. It seems that by the time Augustine wrote his great work on the Trinity, *De Trinitate*, early in the fifth century, the so-called Arians had made it an 'axiom that the one who sends is greater than the one who is sent.'[48] Augustine spends many pages in several sections repudiating the idea that to be sent implies

---

[42] *The Trinity*, 1.1.14 (p. 74)

[43] *The Trinity*, 2.1.2 (p. 98).

[44] *The Trinity*, 2.1.2 (p. 98).

[45] *The Trinity*, 1.314ff (pp. 74ff), 2.1.2-3 (pp. 98-99).

[46] *The Trinity*, 2.1.3 (p. 98).

[47] *The Trinity*, 1.1.1 (p. 65).

[48] *The Trinity*, 2.2.7 (p. 101).

subordination.[49] For him, sending language is human language and it cannot be taken literally when used of God.

Finally, I note that Augustine assumes that the Old Testament is Christian scripture and what is written there speaks beyond its historical meaning. For him, the Hebrew scriptures point to Christ and in particular foreshadow the doctrine of the Trinity, although he accepts that they do not reveal God as triune.[50] In the *City of God*, Augustine writes in reference to the Old Testament, saying we believe, 'Historical events and the narrative of them have always some foreshadowing of things to come, and are always to be interpreted with reference to Christ and his Church.'[51] (He then goes on to say much the same on prophetic texts).

### What we learn from Athanasius and Augustine

In the face of the fact that within scripture there is diversity of teaching and the heretics quote the scriptures in support of their views, Athanasius and Augustine pioneer a way of reading scripture that makes it possible to reach firm theological positions that reflect the teaching of the church as it has developed that are holistically and profoundly scriptural. From them we learn that,

- Confronted with any theological question the first question the theologian should ask is, What has the church in the past come to conclude is the overall teaching of scripture on this matter? The most authoritative answer to this question when it comes to the Trinity and the person of Christ is found in the creeds, and for Protestants in particular on these two matters and may others, in the Reformation and post-Reformation confessions. These guides to the right interpretation of scripture of course cannot contribute anything when there is no weighty exegetical tradition from the past such as with the spiritual gifts, or the male-female relationship,[52] and even possibly the doctrine of the church.

---

[49] *The Trinity*, 2.2.7 (pp.101-102), 2.2.8 (pp. 108) 2.2.9 (p. 108-109), 4.5.25-32 (pp. 171-177).

[50] See his discussion on the theophany's of the Old Testament, *The Trinity* , 2.1.1 to 2.7.35 (pp. 97-122).

[51] *Concerning the City of God Against the Pagans*, translated by H. Betterson (London: Penguin, 1972), 16.2 (p. 652).

[52] Until the 1960's church leaders tended to almost perfectly reflect the prevailing cultural ideas about women, sometimes in very negative terms. There was no deep and profound reflection on the status and ministry of women prior to this time and no creedal or confessional statements on the relationship of the sexes. In other words, there was no weighty tradition to guide the exegetical position.

- In coming to scripture to determine a theological position one or two texts that may possibly reflect what we believe cannot be the basis for what the church should believe. Doctrines should reflect what is primary and consistently taught throughout scripture. The whole 'scope' of scripture is determinative. Text that are patently discordant need to be interpreted in the light of the whole of scriptural revelation. The great Reformed scholar, Oscar Cullmann, goes as far as to say 'the fountainhead of all false biblical interpretation and all heresy is invariably the isolation and absolutising of one single passage.'[53]

- In any theological reading of scripture a hermeneutic suggested by scripture is demanded if 'text-jam' is to be avoided. In other words, a way of reading the diverse comments in scripture on any matter of importance needs to be established. Some hermeneutical rules may universally apply and some may be specific to one doctrine. Athanasius and Augustine lay down the rule applicable to the Trinity; texts that speak of the Son as subordinate and obedient to the Father speak of him in 'the form of a servant' in the time of his earthly ministry: texts that speak of him as God in all power and might speak of him 'in the form of God' as he is in eternity with the Father and the Spirit. In the sixteenth century, the Protestant Reformers saw that with the doctrine of justification by faith, a specific hermeneutical rule was also needed; Paul is primary, James is secondary because he is simply seeking to correct a wrong understanding of Paul. In the contemporary debate on the status and ministry of women, given that we should begin study this question where the Bible begins, Genesis 1 to 3,[54] not with exceptional and disputed texts such as Galatians 3:28 or 1 Timothy 2:11-14, another rule follows. 'All texts that speak of the substantial equality of the two differentiated sexes speak of the creation ideal; all texts that speak of the subordination of women speak of fallen reality (Gen. 3:16); what is not pleasing to God.

---

[53] *The State in the New Testament* (SCM, London, 1963), 47.

[54] It is now generally agreed by scholarly commentators that Gen. 2 does not subordinate the woman. The point of the chapter is that man (the male) is helpless, incomplete alone. He is only man in distinction to woman when his counterpart, Eve, stands by his side, head erect. The subordination of the woman is entirely a consequence of sin and is to be opposed.

- When it comes to the Old Testament the theologian should not limit the meaning of any text to its historical meaning. When the scriptures suggest a christological interpretation we should be open to this, and when an Old Testament text is christologically interpreted by a New Testament author we should embrace that interpretation. Indeed, the theologian should accept that the critical and historical meaning of any text in the Old or New Testament does not necessarily exhaust its meaning.

- Finally, from Athanasius and Augustine the theologian learns that creaturely language used of God is analogical in nature. This is something that the historical and critical study of scripture would never tell us.

**To sum up**

What I have learned from Athanasius and Augustine is that doctrines do not spring immediately from the text of scripture. A way of reading scripture that gives unity to its diverse teaching and that pinpoints what is absolutely central to the issue in question needs to be found to enunciate any doctrine. In discovering this no theologian ever works alone. The theological enterprise is a communal one where each generation of theologians owes something to those before him. Thus to say, 'All I believe comes directly from the Bible' is not really true. The reality is that what we believe as Christians, our doctrines, are in fact the fruit of long and deep reflection on scripture where each theologian is informed and builds on those before him. In this process a way of reading scripture in relation to each doctrine is developed and honed. This given understanding of scripture is the lens through which later theologians read the scriptures as they seek to confirm and possibly refine a specific doctrine. What I have just described, I believe, is the essence of what is called 'the theological interpretation of scripture.'

# Adultery, Divorce, and the Hard-Hearted People of God: The Function of the Matthean Exception Clause (Matt 19:9) in Its Literary Context

David W. Pao

Trinity Evangelical Divinity School, Deerfield, IL, USA

Abstract

*While the interpretation of Matt 19:1-12, and the exception clause in particular, has been a topic of great debate among scholars, the narrative context of Matthew and the broader prophetic and theological contexts in which he was writing have been largely overlooked. This article argues that Matthew is locating this legal exposition of Deut 24:1-4 within a wider prophetic interpretation of the passage: God's covenant people have been unfaithful to their covenant partner, and therefore God has the right to divorce them. This Matthean divorce text therefore plays a significant role in its literary context where both the issues of the identity of God's renewed people and the rejection of God and his prophet by his own people are addressed. A legal discussion of marital unfaithfulness addressed to those who have "hard hearts" (19:8) becomes an indictment of the "wicked and adulterous generation" (12:39; 16:4).*

## Introduction

Jesus' discussion of divorce in Matt 19:1-12 has attracted substantial scholarly attention. Its location in the midst of the synoptic discussions on divorce (Mark 10:1-12; Luke 16:18; cf. Matt 5:31-32) has generated detailed studies on its tradition history.[1] The uniquely Matthean form of the question concerning whether it is lawful to divorce one's wife "for any reason" (κατὰ πᾶσαν αἰτίαν, 19:3) has also firmly located this discussion within Jewish legal discussions, and this Matthean passage has therefore been examined in light of the debate between the schools of Hillel and Shammai concerning

---

[1] E.g. W. Stenger, "Zur Rekonstruktion eines Jesusworts anhand der synoptischen Ehescheidungslogien (Mt 5,32; 19,9; Lk 10,11f [sic]; Mk 10,11f)," *Kairos* 26 (1984), 194-205; H. Hübner, *Das Gesetz in der synoptischen Tradition* (2nd ed.; Göttingen: Vandenhoeck & Ruprecht, 1986), 61-62.

legitimate grounds of divorce.² For those focusing on Matthew's understanding of the Law, this passage has been taken as a direct challenge to the validity of the Law so that to "obey the commandments of the law" is to "disobey the will of God;"³ others, however, see in this passage an attempt to "rescue" the Mosaic Law "from total abolition."⁴

Turning to the concluding verses of this passage, the uniquely Matthean reference to the eunuchs (19:10-12) has also produced divergent readings. Many still adhere to the traditional reading that considers this conclusion as pointing to Jesus' affirmation of a celibate life,⁵ a life that he himself likely lived.⁶ Dissatisfied with this reading, some recent interpreters have seen in these eunuchs a symbol of "shame;" Jesus is therefore calling his disciples to adopt "the values befitting the forthcoming Kingdom" even when they are "stigmatized by others."⁷

---

² E.g. M. D. Goulder, *Midrash and Lection in Matthew* (London: SPCK, 1974), 290-291; D. Instone-Brewer, *Divorce and Remarriage in the Bible: The Social and Literary Context* (Grand Rapids: Eerdmans, 2002), 85-132. Increasing attention has also been directed to other Second-Temple Palestinian sources (e.g. J. R. Mueller, "The Temple Scroll and the Gospel Divorce Texts," *RevQ* 10 [1980], 247-256; P. Sigal, *The Halakah of Jesus of Nazareth According to the Gospel of Matthew* [Lanham, MD: University Press of America 1986], 83-118; J. Kampen, "The Matthean Divorce Texts Re-examined," *New Qumran Texts and Studies: Proceedings of the First Meeting of the International Organization for Qumran Studies, Paris 1992* [ed. G. J. Brooke and F. G. Martínez; STDJ 15; Leiden: Brill, 1994], 149-167).

³ É. Cuvillier, "Torah Observance and Radicalization in the First Gospel. Matthew and First-Century Judaism: A Contribution to the Debate," *NTS* 55 (2009), 144-159; cf. J. P. Meier, *Law and History in Matthew's Gospel: A Redactional Study of Mt. 5:17-48* (AnBib 71; Rome: Biblical Institute Press, 1976), 41-56.

⁴ G. Barth, "Matthew's Understanding of the Law," in G. Bornkamm, G. Barth, and H. J. Held, *Tradition and Interpretation in Matthew* (trans. P. Scott; Philadelphia: Fortress, 1963), 58-164; cf. D. T. Smith, "The Matthean Exception Clauses in the Light of Matthew's Theology and Community," *Studia Biblica et Theologica* 17 (1989), 55-82.

⁵ D. W. Trautman, *The Eunuch Logion of Matthew 19,12: Historical and Exegetical Dimensions as Related to Celibacy* (Rome: Catholic Book Agency, 1966); J. Kodell, "The Celibacy Logion in Matthew 19:12," *BTB* 8 (1978), 19-23.

⁶ F. J. Moloney, "Matthew 19:3-12 and Celibacy: A Redactional and Form Critical Study," *JSNT* 2 (1979), 42-60. Some even consider the Matthean Jesus as rejecting the family (e.g. A. J. Dewey "The Unkindest Cut of All?" *Forum* 8 [1992], 113-122).

⁷ C. Bernabé, "Of Eunuchs and Predators: Matthew 19:1-12 in a Cultural Context," *BTB* 33 (2003), 128-134; cf. J. H. Neyrey, *Honor and Shame in the Gospel of Matthew* (Louisville, KY: Westminster, 1998), 201; L. J. Lawrence, *An Ethnography of the Gospel of Matthew* (WUNT 2.165; Tübingen: Mohr Siebeck, 2003), 275-276. There are also those who consider Jesus using the eunuch-symbol to challenge conceptions of the male-dominated household (e.g. R. Talbott, "Imagining the Matthean Eunuch Community: Kyriarchy on the Chopping Block," *JFSR* 22 [2006], 21-43) or even traditional sexual identities and boundaries (e.g. J. D. Hester, "Eunuchs and the Postgender Jesus: Matthew 19:12 and Transgressive Sexualities," *JSNT* 28 [2005], 13-40).

Scholarly attention on Matt 19:1-12 has, however, focused on the exception clause in v. 9: μὴ ἐπὶ πορνείᾳ. Since it only appears in Matthew, this clause is often considered to be a case of Matthean redaction,[8] although some have suggested that it was found in Matthew's source(s)[9] if not coming from the historical Jesus himself.[10] The exact meaning of μὴ ἐπί has also been debated, but most understand this to be an ellipsis for εἰ/ἐάν μὴ ἐπί; together with παρεκτός of 5:32 the phrase acquires an exceptive sense: "except" or "all but."[11] Whether this exception clause is meant to qualify only the act of divorce in the previous clause[12] or also the act of remarrying in the clause that follows[13] continues to be debated.[14] Even more contentiously debated is the exact meaning of πορνεία, although the majority of commentators continue to take this word as referring to certain acts of sexual unfaithfulness within the marital relationship. This debate will be discussed in more detail in the next section.

While this brief survey of scholarship has demonstrated that that much attention has been devoted to the numerous details within the text and the tradition history behind the text, the literary context and the theological import of this passage in general, and the exception clause in particular, has been ignored. After Matthew's

---

[8] E.g. D. R. Catchpole, "The Synoptic Divorce Material as a Traditio-Historical Problem," *BJRL* 57 (1974), 92-127; R. A. Guelich, *The Sermon on the Mount: A Foundation for Understanding* (Waco, Tex.: Word, 1982), 200; J. D. G. Dunn, "How Did Matthew Go About Composing His Gospel," in *Jesus, Matthew's Gospel and Early Christianity: Studies in Memory of Graham N. Stanton* (ed. D. M. Gurtner, J. Willitts and R. A. Burridge; LNTS 435; London/New York: T&T Clark), 47.

[9] H. D. Betz, *The Sermon on the Mount* (Hermeneia; Minneapolis: Fortress, 1995), 249.

[10] D. Warden, "The Word of Jesus on Divorce," *ResQ* 39 (1997), 141-153.

[11] For a recent challenge to this majority reading, see A. R. Guenther, "The Exception Phrases: Except πορνεία, Including πορνεία, or Excluding πορνεία? [Matthew 5:32; 19:9]," *TynBul* 53 (2002), 83-96, who argues that while παρεκτός in 5:32 does carry an exceptive force ("except"), μὴ ἐπί by itself in 19:9 carries the force of exclusion ("excluding the matter"). This, however, ignores the parallel between the two Matthean passages. Moreover, μὴ ἐπί can indeed be taken as an ellipsis for εἰ/ἐάν μὴ ἐπί, and Guenther admits that this fuller form does carry an exceptive force (95).

[12] D. E. Holwerda, "Jesus on Divorce: An Assessment of a New Proposal," *CTJ* 22 (1987), 114-120; P. H. Wiebe, "Jesus' Divorce Exception," *JETS* 32 (1989), 327-333.

[13] A. Feuillet, "L'indissolubilité du mariage et le monde féminin d'après la doctrine évangélique et quelques autres données bibliques paralliles," *Scripta Theologica* 17 (1985), 415-461; W. A. Heth and G. J. Wenham, *Jesus and Divorce* (Milton Keynes, UK: Paternoster, 2000 [1984]).

[14] Both sides have also appealed to the competing interpretations of this clause in Church Fathers (see J. Moingt, "Le Divorce 'Pour Motif d'Impudicité'," *RSR* 56 [1968], 339-44).

initial treatment of the issue of divorce in 5:31-32 where Jesus' teaching is juxtaposed with the Mosaic Law (as mediated through first-century Jewish teachers),[15] what is the function of this second lengthier treatment of divorce in 19:1-12? How does this divorce discussion contribute to both its immediate (19:1-20:16) and wider contexts (16:21-18:35; 20:17-23:39) in Matthew's Gospel?

As Jesus provides a legal exposition of the Mosaic Law found in Deut 24:1-4, we shall suggest that Matthew is locating this exposition within the wider prophetic interpretation of the same Deuteronomy passage where God's people are accused of being unfaithful to their covenantal partner. As a result of their unfaithfulness, God has the right to divorce them. This Matthean divorce text therefore plays a significant theological role in both its immediate and wider contexts where both the issues of the identity of God's renewed people and the rejection of God and his prophet by his own people are addressed. A legal discussion of marital unfaithfulness addressed to those who have "hard hearts" (19:8) becomes an indictment of the "wicked and adulterous generation" (12:39; 16:4).

Before examining the function of this divorce text within its context, however, we must return to the question of the meaning of πορνεία in 19:9.

## Πορνεία as Adultery

In New Testament and Early Christian literature, the semantic range of πορνεία includes "unlawful sexual intercourse, prostitution, unchastity, fornication" and the "participation in prohibited degrees of marriage."[16] A similar range of possible meanings has been proposed for the reading of πορνεία in Matt 19:9 (cf. 5:32). Several possible definitions can be readily dismissed. Reading Matt 19:9 in light of Lev 21:7, some consider premarital sex as the meaning of πορνεία.[17] In light of the fact that Jesus is dealing with Deuteronomy 24 and not Leviticus 21 here, the relevance of Lev 21:7 must be questioned. Moreover, since the issue

---

[15] The repetitive nature of Jesus' teaching is well illustrated in the complicated textual history behind the two texts. See the discussions in H. Crouzel, "The Synoptic Divorce Material as a Traditio-Historical Problem," *BJRL* 57 (1972), 98-119 and M. W. Holmes, "The Text of the Matthean Divorce Passages: A Comment on the Appeal to Harmonization in Textual Decisions," *JBL* 109 (1990), 651-664.

[16] BDAG, s.v. πορνεία 2.

[17] E.g. A. Isaksson, *Marriage and Ministry in the New Temple* (Lund: Gleerup, 1965), 116-152.

is marriage and grounds for divorce, sexual acts during marriage seem to be in view. Others have proposed the meaning of polygamy,[18] but this would hardly be an issue among the Jews (or Jewish Christians), especially because this exception clause addresses married women, although a prohibition against adultery does effectively rule out polygamy for the men involved.

The remaining three suggestions deserve more serious consideration: incestuous relationships, general sexual immorality, and adultery. First proposed by Joseph Bonsirven,[19] πορνεία as incestuous relationships has gained considerable support among biblical scholars.[20] Similar references can possibly be found in the use of this word in other New Testament documents (e.g. Acts 15:20, 29; 21:25; 1 Cor 5:1) as Gentile believers are to avoid sexual relationships among close relatives as noted in Leviticus 18. Further support is claimed to be found in the Qumran material (cf. CD 5.7-10) where the form of incest being targeted could have been translated as πορνεία in Greek.[21] If so, Matthew might have inserted this exception clause to prevent Gentile converts from remaining in incestuous relationships.

Despite its popularity, this reading is problematic. In its context in Matthew 19, where the legal dispute grounded in the reading of Deut 24:1-4 is addressed, a discussion of incest seems out of place. Moreover, for those in such relationships, a divorce certificate would not have been required because such a marriage would not have been recognized as a valid one.[22] The alleged parallels in Acts 15 and 21 are also questionable since the meaning of πορνεία there should not be limited to incest, especially when it is listed with other moral and cultic prohibitions. More importantly, the word πορνεία does not even appear in Leviticus 18 (LXX), and the parallel discussion in the Qumran material is only limited to one or two

---

[18] E.g. L. Ramaroson, "Une nouvell interprétation de la 'clausule' de Mt 19,9," *ScEs* 23 (1971), 247-251.

[19] J. Bonsirven, *Le divorce dans le Nouveau Testament* (Paris: Desclée, 1948), 46-60.

[20] P. Bonnard, *L'Évangile selon Saint Matthieu* (CNT 1; Neuchatel: Delachaux & Niestlé, 1963), 69-70; Meier, *Law and History in Matthew's Gospel*, 147-150; J. Jensen, "Does *Porneia* Mean Fornication? A Critique of Bruce Malina," *NovT* 20 (1978), 161-184; F. J. Moloney, "Matthew 19:3-12 and Celibacy: A Redactional and Form Critical Study," *JSNT* 2 (1979), 42-60; B. Witherington, III., "Matthew 5.32 and 19.9 – Exception or Exceptional Situation?" *NTS* 31 (1985), 571-576.

[21] J. A. Fitzmyer, "The Matthean Divorce Texts and Some New Palestinian Evidence," *TS* 37 (1976), 197-226.

[22] Cf. Sigal, *Halakah of Jesus of Nazareth*, 100-101.

passages. In terms of historical context, incestuous relationships are rare even among the Gentiles in first-century Mediterranean world,[23] and it is unlikely that it is a prominent concern in the Matthean community if we assume its Syro-Palestinian setting. Finally, this reading relies heavily on the assumption that this is a Matthean insertion that addresses the concern of his community,[24] an assumption that remains to be proven.

Instead of narrowing the meaning of πορνεία to incestuous relationships, others have suggested that this term should be understood in its full semantic range in reference to sexual immorality in general.[25] Those advocating this reading point to the presence of an explicit reference to adultery (μοιχεία) in the same verse, and therefore πορνεία "must be general, not specific."[26] This reading certainly does full justice to the various uses of πορνεία in contemporary Greek literature, but the meaning of any word must be determined by its own context. In this Matthean discussion of divorce, πορνεία must refer to sexual acts that would break the marriage bond, and any such sexual acts may be grouped together under the term "adultery." The use of the term "adultery" does not necessarily reduce πορνεία to one kind of sexual act since it can refer to any sexual acts that are deemed to reflect marital unfaithfulness according to the Mosaic (and Jewish) Law. Its most natural reference lies, however, in an explicit sexual act with someone outside one's legitimate marital relationship.

The understanding of πορνεία as adultery continues to receive strong support among commentators.[27] Several factors further support this reading. First, adultery as the primary grounds for

---

[23] See, in particular, the helpful discussion in C. S. Keener, *A Commentary on the Gospel of Matthew* (Grand Rapids: Eerdmans, 1999), 467-469, who provides detailed evidence that incestuous relationships are widely rejected outside of Egypt, and that "the incest taboo is almost universal" (468).

[24] Cf. A. Yarbro Collins, *Mark* (Hermeneia; Minneapolis: Fortress, 2007), 202-203.

[25] E.g. E. Lövestam, "Divorce and Remarriage in the New Testament," *JLA* 4 (1981), 47-65; D. A. Carson, "Matthew," in T. Longman III and D. E. Garland, *The Expositor's Bible Commentary*, vol. 9 (rev. ed.; Grand Rapids: Zondervan, 2010), 467.

[26] Betz, *Sermon on the Mount*, 250.

[27] T. V. Fleming, "Christ and Divorce," *TS* 24 (1963), 106-20; J. Gnilka, *Das Matthäusevangelium*, I. Teil (HKNT 1; Freiburg: Herder, 1986), 167-169; W. D. Davies and D. C. Allison, Jr., *Matthew*, vol. I (ICC; Edinburgh: T&T Clark, 1988), 530-31; Keener, *Commentary on the Gospel of Matthew*, 466; C. L. Blomberg, "Matthew," in *Commentary on the New Testament Use of the Old Testament* (ed. G. K. Beale and D. A. Carson; Grand Rapids: Baker, 2007), 24, 61.

divorce is well attested in certain groups in pre-Rabbinic Judaism.²⁸ If πορνεία refers to other sexual acts, then Jesus and/or Matthew would have to make this clear. Second, in reference to that which can break the marriage bond, the sexual act(s) involved would by definition be understood as the sin of adultery. Third, since this discussion about divorce is grounded in Deut 24:1-4, and that דבר ערות in Deut 24:1 should best be understood as an illicit sexual act that violates the marital relationship,²⁹ the corresponding term πορνεία in the Matthean divorce texts should carry the same meaning. Finally, the case of Joseph in Matt 1:18-25 provides internal support for this reading since if πορνεία is not understood as referring to adultery, Joseph, who is about "to divorce" (ἀπολῦσαι, cf. 19:9) Mary privately because of her pregnancy, will not be considered as "a righteous/just man" (1:19).³⁰

As to why Matthew would use two different terms (πορνεία, μοιχεία) in reference to the same act of adultery, several explanations are possible. First, the use of these two terms may simply be a case of stylistic variation. A similar case can be identified in Sir 23:23 where the same two word-groups appear in a single sentence: "she committed adultery by an adulterous act" (ἐν πορνείᾳ ἐμοιχεύθη). Even if the two terms have different semantic ranges, in this context, πορνεία can refer to adulterous acts precisely because of its proximity with the μοιχ- word-group. Similar juxtaposition of the two word-groups can also be found in the LXX (e.g. Hos 1:2; 2:4; Jer 3:1, 8-9). Second, it appears that the πορν- word-group is often applied to adulterous acts committed by women, while the μοιχ- word-group by men.³¹ This would fit the uses of the two terms in Matt 19:9. Third, it has also been suggested that the more general term πορνεία may include adulterous acts even during the betrothal period, while μοιχεία specifically refers to

---

[28] M. Bockmuehl, "Matthew 5.32; 19.9 in the Light of Pre-Rabbinic Halakhah," *NTS* 35 (1989), 291-295.

[29] P. Foster, *Community, Law and Mission in Matthew's Gospel* (WUNT 2.177; Tübingen: Mohr Siebeck, 2004), 110-112.

[30] D. C. Allison, Jr., "Divorce, Celibacy and Joseph (Matthew 1.18-25 and 19.1-12)," *JSNT* 49 (1993), 3-10.

[31] F. Hauck and S. Schulz, "Πόρνη κτλ.," *TDNT* 6.592.

adulterous acts during marriage.[32] This would also fit the Matthean context well especially in light of Josephs' act in 1:18-25.

## Adultery and Covenantal Infidelity in the Prophetic Traditions

Πορνεία and its related word-groups play an important role in the prophetic traditions, especially in Jeremiah and Hosea, in the depiction of God's unfaithful covenantal partner. Linguistic and thematic parallels will demonstrate that Matthew is aware of the adultery discourses in these two prophets, and these discourses will in turn illuminate the function of the Matthean adultery-divorce discussion in 19:1-12. Significantly, all three authors ground their discussions in the Mosaic stipulations in Deut 24:1-4.

### Jeremiah and the Adulterous People of God

While Matt 19:1-12 is often taken as addressing a legal matter that affects primarily individual households, embedded in this passage is a critique of those among God's people who refuse to respond to the words and deeds of his Messiah. In 19:8, Jesus claims that Moses allows for the possibility of divorce because of their τὴν σκληροκαρδίαν ("hard hearts").[33] In the canonical sections of LXX, σκληροκαρδία appears only in Deut 10:16 and Jer 4:4,[34] and an allusion to at least one of these two passages is likely because it is found only in the LXX among Greek literature prior to the New Testament.[35] Among the two, the closest in context is Jer 4:4 since both passages (Matt 19:1-12 and Jer 3:1-4:4) deal with the question of divorce and both are grounded in Deut 24:1-4.[36] It has even been

---

[32] Cf. D. Janzen, "The Meaning of *Porneia* in Matthew 5.32 and 19.9: An Approach from the Study of Ancient Near Eastern Culture," *JSNT* 80 (2000), 66-80.

[33] Here, the singular τὴν σκληροκαρδίαν likely functions as a collective singular.

[34] Outside the canonical portions only in Sir 16:10. Other related terms include σκληροκάρδιος (Prov 17:20; Ezek 3:7) and σκληροτράχηλος (Exod 33:3, 5; 34:9; Deut 9:6, 13; Prov 29:1 [cf. Sir 16:11; Bar 2:30]). See the discussion in K. Berger, "Harthezigkeit und Gottes Gesetz: Die Vorgeschichte des antijüdischen Vorwurfs in Mc 10:5," *ZNW* 61 (1970), 1-47.

[35] As confirmed by the *Thesaurus Linguae Graecae* database.

[36] Cf. Instone-Brewer, *Divorce and Remarriage in the Bible*, 145. While a small minority of scholars argues that both Jeremiah 3-4 (esp. 3:1) and Deuteronomy 24 (esp. 24:1-4) independently draw from the same tradition (e.g. T. R. Hobbs, "Jeremiah 3.1-5 and Deuteronomy 24.1-4," *ZAW* 86 [1974], 23-29), many do recognize the dependence of Jeremiah 3-4 on Deuteronomy 24 (e.g. J. D. Martin, "The Forensic Background to Jeremiah iii. 1," *VT* 19 [1969], 82-92; J. R. Lundbom, *Jeremiah 1-20* [AB 21a; New York: Doubleday, 1999], 300). The minor differences between Jer 3:1 and Deut 24:1-4 "occur in the hortatory-

suggested that Jeremiah 3-4 provides the missing link between Deuteronomy 24 and the Matthean discourses on divorce as both expand and qualify the Mosaic legislation on divorce.[37] For this Gospel writer, who has a special interest in the prophet Jeremiah, this connection is perhaps not surprising,[38] even though this teaching is likely rooted in earlier traditions in light of the Markan parallel in 10:5.[39] What has not been shown, however, is the significance of this scriptural allusion for the reading of Matt 19:1-12, especially the uniquely Matthean exception clause in 19:9.

Jer 4:4 is the conclusion of a section that begins in 3:1[40] where the author bases his discussion on the legal material in Deut 24:1-4 concerning the possibility of the return of a divorced wife and then applies such material to God's unfaithful people:

> If a man dismisses his wife
>   and she goes from him
> and becomes another man's,
>   surely, if she returns, she will not return any more to him?
> Surely when she becomes polluted,
>   that woman will be polluted?
> And you have played the whore (ἐξεπόρνευσας) with many shepherds,
>   and would you return to me?
>       says the Lord. (Jer 3:1)[41]

---

paraenetic conclusion, not in the technical and operative sections of the legal topos" (M. Fishbane, *Biblical Interpretation in Ancient Israel* [Oxford: Clarendon, 1988], 311).

[37] M. I. Gruber, "Jeremiah 3:1-4:2 between Deuteronomy 24 and Matthew 5: Jeremiah's Exercise in Ethical Criticism," in *Birkat Shalom: Studies in the Bible, Ancient Near Eastern Literature, and Postbiblical Judaism Presented to Shalom M. Paul on the Occasion of His Seventieth Birthday*, vol. 1 (ed. C. Cohen et al.; Winona Lake, IN: Eisenbrauns, 2008), 239-240, further suggests that Jeremiah is directly quoting from Deut 24:1-4, and לאמר in Jer 3:1 should be rendered as "it is stated in Scripture."

[38] The name "Jeremiah" only appears in Matthew (2:17; 16:14; 27:9) among the New Testament writers. For the wider significance of Jeremiah in Matthew's Gospel, see M. Knowles, *Jeremiah in Matthew's Gospel: The Rejected Prophet Motif in Matthaean Redaction* (JSNTSup 68; Sheffield: JSOT, 1993).

[39] Moving beyond traditional redaction-critical concerns, Matthew's theology should not be limited to only the uniquely Matthean material. The next section on Hosea will show, however, that the uniquely Matthean material does support a further development beyond the Markan material.

[40] One can also trace the beginning of this section to 2:1-9 where the marriage of Israel to her husband YHWH is located in the Sinai event (cf. A. Miglio, "Ordeal, Infidelity, and Prophetic Irony in Jeremiah 2,1-9," *SJOT* 24 [2010], 222-34).

[41] In this article, English translation of the LXX is taken from the *New English Translation of the Septuagint* unless otherwise noted.

In the material that follows, God's people are repeatedly accused of committing adultery. The climax of such accusations comes in Jer 3:8-9 where God threatens to divorce his own people:

> And I saw that for everything in which the settlement of Israel was caught,
>
> in which she committed adultery (ἐμοιχᾶτο),
>
> and I sent her away and gave her a document of divorce,[42]
>
> and faithless Iouda did not fear,
>
> but she too went and played the whore (ἐπόρνευσεν).
>
> And her whoredom (ἡ πορνεία) came to nothing,
>
> and she committed adultery (ἐμοίχευσεν) with tree and stone.

The thematic and linguistic parallels between this passage and Matt 19:9 should not be overlooked. In both one finds both πορν- and μοιχ- word-groups being used to describe adulterous acts. In Jer 3:8-9, the two word-groups are used interchangeably, and this accords well with our explanation of the appearances of these word-groups in Matt 19:9. Furthermore, in the midst of discussing their adulterous acts, the possibility of divorce is raised. When a party commits adultery, the other party has the right to divorce his partner.

This section ends with a final call for God's hard-hearted people to repent:

> Be circumcised to your God,
>
> and remove the foreskin of your hard heart (lit., τὴν σκληροκαρδίαν),
>
> O men of Iouda and inhabitants of Ierousalem,
>
> or else my anger goes forth like fire
>
> and will blaze forth, and there will be no one to quench
>
> because of the evil of your doings. (Jer 4:4)

With the use of the same word (σκληροκαρδία), Jesus likewise accuses the unrepentant people of God for being unfaithful to their

---

[42] NETS has "a document of dismissal" here, but the word ἀποστασίου in this context should be taken as a technical term for a "notice of divorce" (BDAG, s.v. ἀποστάσιον).

partner (Matt 19:8).[43] In light of Jer 3:1-4:4, Jesus' discussion of divorce with the Pharisees in Matt 19:1-12 takes on added significance. The claim that they are hard-hearted becomes an indictment of their unfaithfulness to their God. The exception clause in Matt 19:9 ("except for adultery," μὴ ἐπὶ πορνείᾳ) would therefore provide the grounds upon which God is able to divorce his own people as it is explicitly stated in Jer 3:8-9. A discussion of the relationship between a husband and a wife is then turned into a description of the relationship between God and his unrepentant covenantal partner. In support of this reading, we must turn to another label that is applied to the God's unrepentant people in Matthew: "evil and adulterous generation."

### Hosea and the Adulterous People of God

Further support for the understanding of God's unrepentant people in marital terms can be found in the unique Matthean label: πονηρὰ καὶ μοιχαλίς ("evil and adulterous generation," Matt 12: 39; γενεὰ 16:4). As in the label of σκληροκαρδία in 19:9, this label is also applied to the Pharisees and their companions. In the New Testament, πονηρός used together with μοιχαλίς[44] can only be found in Matthew.[45] In the LXX, this phrase appears only once in Hos 3:1, in a context identical to that of Jer 3:1-4:4 where God's people are again described as being unfaithful to their covenantal partner:

> And the Lord said to me,
>
> "Go again, and love a woman
>
> who loves evil things and is an adulteress (πονηρὰ καὶ μοιχαλίν),
>
> just as God loves the sons of Israel,

---

[43] The motif of hard-heartedness is frequently applied to God's people when they were disobedient to God's commandments (Berger, "Harthezigkeit und Gottes Gesetz," 43). In Matt 19:1-12, while the focus is on the Mosaic stipulations of Deut 24:1-4, this motif is also applied to their rebellion against God's created order (cf. vv. 4-5). Both aspects can also be found in relations to this theme in Second Temple Jewish literature (cf. *1 En.* 1:9-54; 5:4; see L. Doering, "Marriage and Creation in Mark 10 and CD 4-5," in *Echoes from the Caves: Qumran and the New Testament* [ed. F. G. Martínez; STDJ 85; Leiden/Brill, 2009], 159-160).

[44] Here, the noun μοιχαλίς ("adulteress") functions as an adjective ("adulterous").

[45] Our focus in this section is limited to πονηρός and μοιχαλίς. For a helpful discussion of γενεά, see E. Lövestam, *Jesus and 'This Generation': A New Testament Study* (trans. M. Linnarud; Stockholm: Almqvist & Wiksell, 1995), 18-36, who examines this term against the flood and wilderness typologies.

> but they turn their attention to foreign gods,
>
> and they like cakes with raisins." (Hos 3:1)

Unlike Mark's τῇ γενεᾷ ταύτῃ τῇ μοιχαλίδι καὶ ἁμαρτωλῷ ("this adulteress and sinful generation," Mark 8:38), the Matthean phrase matches both the wording and the word order of Hos 3:1. Therefore, it is unlikely that the Matthean version is simply a variation of the Markan.[46] Moreover, uniquely Matthean quotations from Hosea (cf. Matt 2:15; 9:13; 12:7) also point to Matthew's knowledge of and interest in this prophet. The fact that this phrase is used twice in Matthew's Gospel (12:39; 16:4) also points to its significance in the depiction of the unfaithful people of God.

Throughout Hosea, πορνεία is used to described God's unfaithful people (Hos 1:2; 2:4[2], 6[4]; 4:11, 12; 6:10), a people who are described as possessed by πνεῦμα πορνείας (lit. "a spirit of adultery," Hos 5:4). As in the case of Jer 3:1-4:4, the discussion of divorce in Hosea is built on Deut 24:1-4.[47] Equally important is the likelihood that Jeremiah is dependent on Hosea in his application of the adultery/divorce imagery to God's unfaithful people.[48] In light of this interrelatedness among the prophets in their use of the Mosaic stipulations in Deut 4:1-4, it should no longer be surprising that Matthew would develop similar themes in his use of the scriptural passages especially in light of his interests in Hosea and Jeremiah.[49]

## Adultery as Covenantal Infidelity

In the above discussion, the linguistic and thematic parallels between Matthew and certain prophetic traditions have been

---

[46] Cf. Collins, *Mark*, 411.

[47] See W. L. Holladay, *Jeremiah 1* (Hermeneia; Philadelphia: Fortress, 1986), 112. See, in particular, Hos 5:4a: "Their deeds do not permit them to return to their God" (cf. Deut 24:4).

[48] See Fishbane, *Biblical Interpretation in Ancient Israel*, 311-312; M. Schulz-Rauch, *Hosea und Jeremia: Zur Wirkungsgeschichte des Hoseabuches* (CTM A16; Stuttgart: Calwer, 1996). It should be noted, however, that both authors develop this imagery in their unique ways, see S. Moughtin-Mumby, *Sexual and Marital Metaphors in Hosea, Jeremiah, Isaiah, and Ezekiel* (Oxford: Oxford University Press, 2008), 49-116.

[49] In the prophetic traditions, the understanding of adultery as covenantal infidelity is of course not limited to Hosea and Jeremiah (cf. Isa 50:1; Ezek 16, 23, 43), but it is primarily in these two works that one finds a clear use of Deut 24:1-4 in the detailed exposition of the possibility of God divorcing his covenantal partner.

established. In light of the prevalent use of the adultery imagery to express covenantal infidelity in these prophetic traditions that Matthew uses, it is at least possible that the divorce/adultery discussion in Matt 19:1-12 is also meant to serve as an indictment of God's unfaithful people. As a husband is allowed to divorce his wife because of adultery, God can also divorce his "evil and adulterous" covenantal partner if they continue to have "hard hearts." Whether this is a viable reading of Matt 19:1-12 can only be determined by the context in which it is situated.

Before turning to the literary context of Matt 19:1-12, a word of clarification has to be provided concerning such use of the πορνεία imagery. This use of the πορνεία imagery builds on the definition of πορνεία as adultery. As noted above, this use of the adultery imagery is already present in the unique Matthean phrase, "evil and adulterous generation" (12:39; 16:4). The question as to whether a discourse on (literal) adultery can carry an additional layer of meaning is answered by Matt 5:27-28:

> You have heard that it was said:
>
> "Do not commit adultery (οὐ μοιχεύσεις)."
>
> But I say to you that anyone who looks at a woman to lust over her
>
> has already committed adultery (ἐμοίχευσεν) with her in his heart.

In this saying, Jesus makes it clear that adultery should never be understood simply as a physical act. In other words, the adultery involved in lusting over a woman refers not only to a "metaphorical" sense of violating the woman, but also an "actual" violation of God's covenant because adultery is "not just a private matter" in the scriptural traditions.[50] A clear distinction between physical adultery and spiritual adultery therefore often cannot and should not be made.

Moreover, in the Jewish scriptures, marriage itself is often understood in covenantal terms. This is particularly clear in Mal 2:10-16 where the covenantal nature of marriage (and divorce) is most clearly articulated.[51] Marriage (and divorce) can in turn be understood as a "metaphorical" expression of covenantal

---

[50] Lövestam, "Divorce and Remarriage in the New Testament," 59.

[51] Cf. G. H. Hugenberger, *Marriage as a Covenant: Biblical Law and Ethics as Developed from Malachi* (VTSup 52; Leiden: Brill, 1994).

faithfulness (and unfaithfulness). Within this theological framework, the understanding of adultery as covenantal infidelity can no longer be considered merely as a secondary extension of the physical act of marital infidelity.

## Matthew 19:1-12 within its Literary Context

Understanding Jesus' discourse on adultery and divorce as addressing also the covenantal infidelity of God's people would explain the function of Matt 19:1-12 in its literary context. Matt 19:1-12 falls within the larger section of 19:1-20:16.[52] The exact thematic connection among the various passages within this section remains, however, unclear to many. Ulrich Luz readily suggests that "there is no apparent systematic arrangement of the scenes, which themselves are formally different and are of varying lengths."[53] Others simply consider this as a transition section with "loosely connected episodes": "it serves as summary of all that has preceded it, and at the same time as introduction to the final events and concluding teaching of the ministry."[54] For those who see a unifying theme, a general umbrella term such as "everyday existence" has often been applied to this section.[55] These labels point to the presence of diverse material in this section, but they are insufficient in explaining why it is situated between a section that centers on ecclesiological concerns (16:21-18:35) and a section that depicts Jesus' final approach into Jerusalem (20:17-23:39).

More promising is the proposal of Warren Carter who argues that this section should be read in light of the ancient *Haustafeln*:[56]

      19:1-2           Transition

---

[52] We consider statements concerning Jesus' journey to Jerusalem as markers of major sections in the second half of Matthew (cf. 16:21; 17:22; 19:1; 20:17; see Wilhelm Wilkens, "Die Komposition des Matthäus-Evangeliums," *NTS* 31 [1985], 24-38; J. Nolland, *The Gospel of Matthew: A Commentary on the Greek Text* [NIGTC; Grand Rapids: Eerdmans, 2005], 763). Although consensus is lacking as to where exactly our present section ends, this would not affect our present analysis since we will also consider the wider context of Matthew's Gospel below.

[53] U. Luz, *Matthew 8-20* (trans. J. E. Crouch; Hermeneia; Minneapolis: Fortress, 2001), 484.

[54] W. F. Albright and C. S. Mann, *Matthew* (AB 26; New York: Doubleday, 1971), 227.

[55] W. D. Davies and D. C. Allison, Jr., *Matthew*, vol. III (ICC; Edinburgh: T&T Clark, 1997), 27.

[56] W. Carter, *Households and Discipleship: A Study of Matthew 19-20* (JSNTSup 103; Sheffield: JSOT, 1994), 56-160; *Matthew and the Margins: A Socio-Political and Religious Reading* (JSNTSup 204; Sheffield: Sheffield Academic Press, 2000), 376-398. Commenting on the Markan parallel in 10:1-31, Anderson (1976) has earlier proposed that the shorter Markan section should also be read in light of the Greco-Roman *Haustafeln*.

| | |
|---|---|
| 19:3-12 | Marriage and Divorce |
| 19:13-15 | Children |
| 19:16-30 | Wealth |
| 20:1-16 | Householder and Laborers[57] |

This structure corresponds to Aristotle's discussion of the household as he deals with husbands and wives, fathers and children, masters and slaves, and also wealth and possessions (*Pol.* 1.1253b).[58] This organization not only provides a coherent structure to the diverse material in Matt 19:1-20:16, it also points to the ecclesiological significance of this section since household discussions often carry political overtones when the household in these traditions is considered "the basic unit of a state or kingdom or city, and a microcosm of imperial society."[59]

Although particular aspects of this proposal can be challenged, it does point to the significance of these household relationships for the discussion of the nature of God's household. Carter himself recognizes that the discussions about children, wealth, and slaves are not simply discussions about domestic matters, but they provide a new model for the structure of God's renewed people: "all disciples are children, there are no parents (19:13-15); following Jesus, not procuring wealth and status, defines discipleship (19:16-30); all disciples are slaves like Jesus, there are no masters (20:17-28)."[60] While the ecclesiological implications for all these relationships are well noted, it is surprising that Carter limits the discussion of marriage and divorce to the domestic level:

---

[57] Carter, *Household and Discipleship*, 193; *Matthew and the Margins*, 376, who considers this section as ending at 20:34, takes 20:1-16 as dealing with the "Parable of the Householder" and the next dealing with slaves (20:17-28). Taking 20:16 as the conclusion of our present chapter, 20:1-16 can also be understood as dealing with both householders and those serving under them.

[58] This basic structure survives in the Hellenistic codes (Dio Chrysostom 5.348-51; Seneca, *Ep.* 94.1; Dionysius of Halicarnassus, *Ant. rom.* 2.25.4-26.4).

[59] Carter, *Matthew and the Margins*, 377. For a further discussion of both the conventional and subversive uses of the Greco-Roman *Haustafel* traditions in the New Testament, see M. Y. MacDonald, "Beyond Identification of the Topos of Household Management: Reading the Household Codes in Light of Recent Methodologies and Theoretical Perspectives in the Study of the New Testament," *NTS* 57 (2010), 65-90.

[60] Carter, *Matthew and the Margins*, 377. As noted above, Carter considers 20:17-28 to be part of the section that begins with 19:1. Discussion of the attitude of the laborers in 20:1-16 would fit well within the paradigm of ancient *Haustafeln* since, like the slaves, the laborers in the parable can only be obedient to the householder who has the right to determine the reward to be given to them.

"Husbands are not to rule over wives but to participate in a 'one-flesh' relationship (19:3-12)."[61]

If the discussions on children, wealth, and slaves point further to aspects of the reality of God's renewed people, the section on marriage and divorce (19:1-12) may carry a similar ecclesiological function. Our discussion about divorce and adultery within the covenantal framework would fit well into this context. Matt 19:1-12 is not simply a general challenge to the cultural norms of gender relationships of the day, it provides specific ecclesiological application in the context of Matthew's Gospel. As God's people continue to refuse to respond to the gospel Jesus is proclaiming, they are threatened to be separated from their covenantal partner, since divorce is indeed possible when γενεὰ πονηρὰ καὶ μοιχαλίς (12:39; 16:4) is immersed in πορνεία (19:9).

The emphasis on the Jewish leaders as representing the unrepentant people of God appears at the beginning of this section where it is noted that the Pharisees came to Jesus for the purpose of "testing" (πειράζοντες, 19:3) him. This "testing" vocabulary not only ties the work of the Pharisees with that of the devil in 4:1, 3, it also ties this passage with 16:1-4 when "the Pharisees and Sadducees came to Jesus to test (πειράζοντες) him." In response Jesus labeled them an "evil and adulterous generation" (γενεὰ πονηρὰ καὶ μοιχαλίς, 16:4). It is precisely to this "evil and adulterous generation" that Jesus issues his accusation against them for their infidelity to their God in 19:1-12.

This reading is also confirmed by the content of 19:1-20:16 where the motif of rebellion against God and his Messiah dominates this section that contains a series of controversy stories.[62] The ecclesiological import of this section in the sense of a critique against God's unrepentant people cannot be denied especially with the presence of 19:28: "Truly I tell you: when all things are renewed, when the Son of Man sits on his glorious throne, you who have followed me will also sit on the twelve thrones, judging the twelve tribes of Israel." In whatever manner this verse is to be taken, it touches on the relationship between Israel and those who are responding to the proclamation of Jesus. The repeated notes on the reversal of "the first" and "the last" in 19:30 and 20:16 provide

---

[61] Carter, *Matthew and the Margins*, 377.

[62] D. Patte, *The Gospel According to Matthew: A Structural Commentary on Matthew's Gospel* (Valley Forge, PA: Trinity Press International, 1987), 262-63.

further coherence to the various episodes in this section as God challenges his people not to rely on their assumed status before him.[63]

While a complete examination of 19:1-20:16 will not be possible, these few observations are sufficient to highlight the overarching concerns of this section. As God's unfaithful partner continues to rebel against him, Jesus points forward to the nature of the renewed people of God. It is within this context that 19:1-12 plays a critical role as it serves as a warning against God's unrepentant people: if they continue to be unfaithful to their God, their God has the right to sever his relationship with them. As in the prophetic traditions, however, this "threat" aims not as a final indictment, but a call for God's people to return (cf. Jer 4:4).

### Matthew 16:21-18:35; 20:17-23:39

This reading of 19:1-20:16 in general and 19:1-12 in particular also fits well within the wider context of Matthew's Gospel. 19:1-20:16 is connected with its context through the travel note at the beginning of this section:

> When Jesus finished these sayings, he left Galilee and went to the region of Judea beyond the Jordan River. (19:1)

This note situates this entire section within Jesus' journey to Jerusalem, and the purpose of this journey is stated in the verse that introduces the preceding section (16:21-18:35):

> From that time on Jesus began to show his disciples that it is necessary for him to go to Jerusalem and suffer many things at the hands of the elders, chief priests, and teachers of the law, and be killed, and on the third day be raised. (16:21)

---

[63] The intended references behind "the first" and "the last" remains unclear. While they can refer to different groups within the church (Luz, *Matthew 8-20*, 536; Nolland, *Gospel of Matthew*, 813) or a general critique against those who are proud (D. Marguerat, *Le Jugement dans l'Evangile de Matthieu* [Genève: Labor et Fides, 1981], 460; K. R. Snodgrass, *Stories with Intent: A Comprehensive Guide to the Parables of Jesus* [Grand Rapids: Eerdmans, 2008], 371), in light of the critique of God's unrepentant people throughout this section, it is still possible to see this as a reference to those who remain unfaithful to God versus the renewed people of God including both Jews and Gentiles who respond to the gospel (R. A. Gundry, *The Sermon on the Mount: A Foundation for Understanding* [Waco, TX: Word, 1982], 399; B. B. Scott, *Hear Then the Parable: A Commentary on the Parables of Jesus* [Minneapolis: Fortress 1989], 297; D. A. Hagner, *Matthew 14-28* (WBC; Dallas, TX: Word, 1993), 573; R. T. France, *The Gospel of Matthew* [NICNT; Grand Rapids: Eerdmans, 2007], 746). In any case, the theme of reversal is clear, and an implied critique of the Jewish leaders who continue to oppose Jesus cannot be denied.

In light of this note, Jesus' travel note in 19:1 should not simply be taken as a geographical note, it aims at situating the entire section within Jesus' journey to suffer and be rejected by his own people.

At the beginning of the next section (20:17-23:39), one again finds a travel note that repeats the same theme of suffering and rejection:

> As Jesus was going up to Jerusalem, he took the twelve disciples aside privately and said to them on the way, "We are going up to Jerusalem and the Son of Man will be handed over to the chief priests and the teachers of the law. They will condemn him to death." (20:17-18)

Our present section is therefore located between two sections that are framed by references to Jesus' suffering and rejection.

In 16:21-18:35, the christological note on the suffering Messiah (16:1-17:20) provides the context for the ecclesiological discussion on the nature and behavior of God's renewed community (17:22-18:35). These twin emphases continue in 20:17-23:39 where one finds the Messiah rejected by his people as he approaches and enters Jerusalem (20:17-21:22) followed by a lengthy series of controversy stories (21:23-22:46) that climax in the woes against the Jewish leaders (23:1-39). Framed by these two sections, it is only to be expected that 19:1-20:16 likewise contain these two emphases. The *Haustafel* structure highlights the ecclesiological significance of the various passages within this section, but the rejection motif is also present through the consistent application of the reversal principle as explicitly noted in 19:30 and 20:16. As both the previous and following sections begin with a note on Jesus being rejected by his own people, this section likewise begins with a section that reinforces this motif (19:1-12). In response to the hard-hearted people (19:8) who continue to test him (19:3), Jesus issues a direct challenge that is embedded in the uniquely Matthean exception clause (19:9): as a husband cannot divorce his wife except for adultery, God would not abandon his people unless they continue to be unfaithful to him. 19:1-12 is therefore not simply an expansion of the legal discussion introduced in 5:31-32, it carries an additional force in this part of Matthew's Gospel as Jesus travels to Jerusalem to be rejected by his own people.[64] A legal discussion becomes an indictment and warning for God's unrepentant people.

---

[64] See, in particular, J. C. Anderson, "Matthew: Sermon and Story," in *Treasures New and Old: Contributions to Matthean Studies* (ed. D. R. Bauer and M. A. Powell; Atlanta: Scholars Press, 1996), 238, who correctly notes that 19:1-12 is not simply concerned with the presentation of

## Conclusion

In light of the linguistic and thematic parallels between Matt 19:1-12 and the prophetic traditions, it is suggested that the uniquely Matthean exception clause in 19:9 should be understood as a warning of the possibility of God divorcing those among his covenantal people who remain unfaithful to him.[65] This reading is confirmed by an examination of Matt 19:1-12 within its immediate and wider contexts in Matthew's presentation of the story of Jesus. As in the prophetic traditions, however, this warning serves ultimately as a call for God's unfaithful people to repent. Matt 19:1-12 therefore does not simply provide yet another abstract discussion of the details of the Law, it becomes both an indictment against God's unfaithful partner and a call to this partner to provide the proper response to God and his Messiah.

---

the correct interpretation of the law, but it is a presentation of the Jewish leaders aligning with the devil in rejecting Jesus.

[65] Although Jeremiah does consider the possibility of God divorcing his (entire) people, the remnant motif embedded in the later sections of his writings (cf. Jer 6:6-9; 23:1-8; 31:2-14; 40:1-45:5; 50:21-46) does point to the presence of those who would continue to be God's covenantal partner. In a similar way, one finds a division among God's people in Matthew although a remnant motif is not explicitly developed in this Gospel.

# The Knowledge of God in St. Basil's De Spiritu Sancto

Murray Hogg

Independent Scholar, Melbourne

Abstract

*Basil of Caesarea's (ca. 329-379CE) De Spiritu Sancto (374CE) is examined in order to ascertain Basil's understanding of epistemology or, more narrowly, his understanding of what is involved in the Christian's knowledge of God. First, the importance of knowledge to Basil is considered with consideration given to the relation to Christian discipleship and the Triune nature of God. Second, the sources of knowledge as described by Basil are considered. Testimony (written and unwritten) and the Holy Spirit are found to be of central importance. Third, the relationship between the various elements of knowledge are examined followed by, fourth, a more detailed look at how the Holy Spirit is involved in Christian the formation of knowledge. Here it is suggested that Basil's epistemology is non-reductionist, holistic, and coherentist in nature. Fifth, the role of epistemic virtue is considered. Finally, the study ends with some consideration of the important consequences which follow from its findings.*

## Introduction

Basil of Caesarea (ca. 329-379CE) was one of three "Cappadocian Fathers" who, in the second half of the fourth century, were central to a major debate over the status of the Holy Spirit. This debate arose in the wake of the council of Nicea (325CE) which had addressed the status of the Son, but had left open the question of the status of the Spirit. It was in the wake of Nicea, then, that Basil's use of those forms of doxology which ascribed equal status to Father, Son, and Holy Spirit was questioned. *De Spiritu Sancto* (374CE, hereafter *DSS*) was his response. (§3)[1]

---

[1] Citations are by section number and are taken from Jackson's venerable yet readily available translation of 1894: *Basil: Letters and Select Works*, ed. Philip Schaff and Henry Wace, trans. Blomfield Jackson, 14 vols., A Select Library of the Christian Church: Nicene and Post-Nicene Fathers: Second Series. 8 (Peabody, MA: Hendrickson, 2004). Johnston's Greek text (Basil of Caesarea, *The Book of Saint Basil the Great, Bishop of Cappadocia, on the Holy Spirit: Written to Amphilochius, Bishop of Iconium, Against the Pneumatomachi*, ed. Charles Francis Harding Johnston (Oxford: Clarendon Press, 1892),

Over and above pneumatology, *DSS* provides insight into Basil's understanding of epistemology. At points we see Basil make quite explicit comment on knowledge. More often, however, his epistemology is implicit and needs to be drawn out. The current paper seeks to investigate the knowledge of God in *DSS* by considering this explicit and implicit commentary.

Here I continue a project begun in an earlier post-graduate thesis where a similar approach was taken in the investigation of John's Gospel.[2] In simple terms the project aims to address the problem of subjectivity in religious truth claims, the idea, crudely put, that religious faith may be affirmed as a matter of subjective belief, but not as a matter of objective knowledge. The issues here are complex, but to cite my earlier investigation: "the need is for an epistemic principle consistent with Christian faith, yet which is in no way open to a charge of subjectivity."[3]

*DSS* fits into this project in as much as it provides an insight into one highly significant Christian thinker's grasp of how knowledge of God is acquired and so serves the purpose of identifying epistemic principle(s) "consistent with Christian faith."

## The Importance of Knowledge in De Spiritu Sancto

### The Categories of Knowledge

At least three categories of knowledge can be found in *DSS*: propositional, tacit, and relational knowledge. They do not receive equal coverage but are all important and in some respects mutually supporting. Knowledge for Basil is important for upon it depends one's Christian growth and, ultimately, one's salvation. Indeed, reading *DSS* it becomes clear that "to be saved" and "to know God" are inseparable. Here I consider the different categories of knowing and their importance.

---

http://archive.org/details/bookofsaintbasil00basi.) was consulted but there was no need to consider the nuances of the original language here.

[2] Murray Hogg, "The Knowledge of God: John's Gospel and Contemporary Epistemology" (Master of Theology, Melbourne School of Theology, 2011), http://postgrad.mst.edu.au/sites/postgrad.mst.edu.au/files/Murray%20Hogg%20The%20Knowledge%20of%20God.pdf.

[3] Ibid., 1.

*Propositional Knowledge*

Whilst *DSS* was prompted by a defence of a particular liturgical practice, that defence depends upon the truth of a particular proposition, namely that the Holy Spirit shares full equality with the Father and the Son. Many other propositional claims are integral to Basil's argument. For instance, Basil's assessment of Aetius' claim that "Whatever...the relation of these terms to one another, such will be the relation of the natures indicated by them." (§4) Basil counters this proposition with a further one: "Scripture varies its expressions as occasion requires, according to the circumstances of the case." (§6) There are also propositions which relate to the knowledge of God ("The superior remoteness of the Father is really inconceivable," §14) and this is particularly apparent when one considers Basil's citations of scripture ("There is one God and Father of whom are all things," §7). In short, every declarative sentence in *DSS*, and there are many such sentences, amounts to evidence that Basil affirms the value of propositional knowledge to Christian faith.

*Tacit Knowledge*

A second form of knowledge can be found in Basil's understanding that:

> The acquisition of true religion is just like that of crafts; both grow bit by bit; apprentices must despise nothing. If a man despise the first elements as small and insignificant, he will never reach the perfection of wisdom. (§2)

Just as a master guides the apprentice through the acquisition of the necessary skills so Basil sees the mature believer taking an interest in the less advanced "toiling at his side as he presses onward to perfection." (§2) *DSS* is itself an example of just this. Such an apprenticeship occurs within a living tradition—a vital aspect of apprenticeship in a craft for once there remains no master to instruct others, the knowledge of that craft is, for all practical purposes, lost.

Knowledge of this sort and its transmission were investigated at length by philosopher of science Michael Polanyi.[4] Such knowledge Polanyi called tacit knowledge and, like Basil, used the example of apprenticeship to explain how such knowledge is replicated. Polanyi wrote: "An art which cannot be specified in detail cannot

---

[4] See particularly Michael Polanyi, *Personal Knowledge: Towards a Post-Critical Philosophy* (Chicago, IL: University of Chicago Press, 1974).

be transmitted by prescription, since no prescription for it exists. It can be passed on only by example from master to apprentice."[5] Consider, for instance, learning to play piano. This cannot happen merely by reading a book, one actually has to sit at a piano and practice. Of course, much can be specified regarding piano playing, but ultimately playing piano and prescribing how to play are quite distinct. Thus, although there is clear emphasis upon propositional knowledge in *DSS*, the knowledge of God clearly extends beyond propositional knowledge to encompass tacit knowledge.

*Relational Knowledge*

Over and above propositional and tacit knowledge *DSS* suggests the knowledge of God involves something like that knowing which occurs in inter-personal relationships. But what does such knowledge involve?

McAdams suggests that to know a person well we must:

> ...obtain data from three distinct and nonoverlapping levels or domains—dispositional traits, personal concerns, and life stories. The three levels provide three very different formats and frameworks for describing a person.[6]

Here "traits" are those behaviours and attitudes that characterise a person, personal concerns are what motivate their actions, and life stories provide the broader narrative which make sense of the whole. McAdams notes that such an account is not actually sufficient to fully account for the knowledge of persons.[7] In addition, there are well-known problems involved in ascribing person-hood to God. McAdams's tripartite schema is nevertheless helpful in that it helps us to see the explicit or implicit indications of divine person-hood in *DSS*. For instance, Basil speaks of:

> the variety of the effectual working which, out of His tender-heartedness to His own creation, according to the peculiar necessity of each, He bestows upon them that need. (§17)

Here we have mention of a trait (tender heartedness) and a concern (for the creation) both of which are set within the context of a life story or narrative (salvation history). In as much as *DSS* portrays

---

[5] Ibid., 53.

[6] Dan P McAdams, "What Do We Know When We Know a Person?," *Journal of Personality* 63, no. 3 (1995): 387, doi:10.1111/j.1467-6494.1995.tb00500.x.

[7] Ibid.

God as having traits, concerns, and a "life story" we can speak of Basil ascribing person-hood to God.

Now these three criteria—traits, concerns, and story—are means by which we can describe a person and this constitutes a necessary aspect of knowing a person: "to know [a person] well...is to describe her fully to another."[8] But it does not seem that description is sufficient for we more often tend to say we "know" a person (and they "know" us) when we can claim to have had a personal encounter with them. The deeper that encounter the stronger our claim to knowledge. This suggests that knowledge of persons is dynamic and a relational concept which centres around the notion of ongoing encounter. McAdams points to this when he speaks of people who "we would like to get to know much better in the future."[9] Such persons will doubtlessly come to know us better too and it seems we cannot properly be said to "know" a person unless they too claim to "know" us. To know a person in the fullest sense is, therefore, to have a dynamic, ongoing, and reciprocal relationship.

To what extent does *DSS* understand our relationship with God in these terms? I discuss below that *DSS* portrays our knowledge of God as dynamic. It is certainly ongoing with the ultimate end being a share in "eternal glory." (§36) The only significant question is whether *DSS* regards our knowledge of God as reciprocal. Now, to suggest that humans have a capacity to know God which exceeds the divine capacity to know humans seems ludicrous. Particularly so given that the epistemic capacities of humans are themselves a matter of divine gift. Consequently, it is appropriate that *DSS* speaks of the soul having "close relationship with God" (§23), of believers being made "spiritual by fellowship with himself" (§23), and, ultimately, "abiding in God" (§23). Whatever the problems associated with the idea of divine person-hood, it seems correct to suggest relational knowledge as the third kind of knowledge, alongside propositional and tacit knowledge, presented in *DSS*.

### Knowledge and Christian Discipleship

Whilst knowledge of God is the end of Christian faith, the believer still has some knowledge of God from the outset. For instance,

---

[8] Ibid., 369.

[9] Ibid., 366.

Basil speaks of the tradition "which bestowed [past tense] on me the boon of the knowledge of God" (§26), invokes Colossians to contrast believers with "them that have not the knowledge of the only begotten" (§9), and speaks of "the knowledge of faith which leads to salvation." (§44) Equally, however, Basil states that the Son is guiding the believer toward the knowledge of God (§19) and such knowledge is the "blessed end" of Christian faith (§18).

In one respect we have here nothing more than an acknowledgement that one can "know" a thing (or person) without having comprehensive knowledge. Yet there is an important aspect to Basil's treatment, namely the direct connection he draws between knowledge and Christian growth: "what is set before us is, so far as is possible with human nature, to be made like unto God. Now without knowledge there can be no making like." (§2) Further, the believer's "advance to perfection" is made "stage by stage" through "the illumination of knowledge." (§18)

If we keep in mind that *DSS* has a multi-facet view of knowledge, and particularly the importance of relational knowledge, there is little problem here. All human relationships involve a similar tension between "knowing" and "not knowing" a person. Newly weds, for instance, "know" one another, but hardly in the way they will after 50 years of marriage. The new believer thus "knows" God in as much as they stand in saving relationship to him, whilst over time that knowledge will deepen until, in the eschaton, current epistemic constraints will fall away. Basil's understanding of Christian knowledge is therefore intimately connected with Basil's understanding of Christian discipleship and even Christian eschatology. Christian knowledge and Christian discipleship, like all of history, are goal directed.

**The Trinitarian Nature of Knowledge**
Fundamental to Basil's understanding of the role played by the Holy Spirit as epistemic agent is the equality of the Spirit with the Father and the Son. The knowledge of God does not come "through the Spirit, but by the Spirit" (§47) who "in Himself...shows the glory of the Only begotten." (§47) Important here is that Basil is combating the idea of sub-numeration, the idea that speaking of "first," "second," and "third" demonstrates a distinction in essence. Those who argue it does "are importing the polytheism of heathen error" (§47) in as much as they deny the

"communion of Nature" (§47) (i.e. the shared divine nature) of the members of the Trinity. Because the Spirit shares in the divine nature, he is more than merely a messenger but will "show thee in Himself the image of the invisible." (§23)

The knowledge of God in *DSS* is thus intimately associated with the full equality of the Spirit and so Trinitarian in nature:

> The way of the knowledge of God lies from One Spirit through the One Son to the One Father, and conversely the natural Goodness and the inherent Holiness and the royal Dignity extend from the Father through the Only-begotten to the Spirit. Thus there is both acknowledgment of the hypostases and the true dogma of the Monarchy is not lost. (§47)

Basil here brings together the individuation of the Father, Son, and Spirit, whilst affirming their full equality. Precisely because they are three separate hypostases but one nature, it becomes possible for the Spirit and Son to mediate the knowledge of the Father, whilst the believer's knowledge of God remains immediate.

## The Sources of Knowledge

### The Standard Account

Basil places great emphasis upon scripture and tradition as sources of knowledge. But a consideration of contemporary epistemology will help us to say more. Here consider Audi's five-fold classification of the sources of knowledge (hereafter called "the standard view"):[10]

- Perception – the senses (sight, hearing, touch, taste, smell) by which we know the sensible world.

- Reason – by which we know abstract entities and their inter-relationships.

- Introspection – by which we know our own inner lives.

- Memory – by which we recall that which we have learned in the past.

---

[10] See part one of Robert Audi, *Epistemology: A Contemporary Introduction to the Theory of Knowledge*, Routledge Contemporary Introductions to Philosophy 2 (London: Routledge, 1998). For a similar analysis, wherein the term "the standard view" is employed, see Richard Feldman, *Epistemology*, ed. Tom L. Beauchamp, Foundations of Philosophy (Upper Saddle River, NJ: Prentice Hall, 2003), 3–4.

- Testimony – by which we have access to knowledge originally acquired by others.

As I have discussed elsewhere[11] there are shortcomings in this account when it comes to the analysis of religious knowledge. One response to such shortcomings is to extend the idea of perception to cover those experiences in which a person takes God to be present to their awareness in a manner analogous to that of sense perception.[12] There are philosophical complexities here but as the present aim is to determine rather than critique the epistemology of *DSS* I will lay them aside. The question at this juncture is this: to which of the above sources of knowledge does *DSS* make appeal?

## The Sources of Knowledge in De Spiritu Sancto

Throughout *DSS* we find reference to the Holy Spirit in connection with the knowledge of God, frequent appeals to scripture and tradition, and appeal to the Fathers of the church (see particularly §72-§74). In addition, Basil states that knowledge can come "through me or others" (§79) with *DSS* itself being a case in point. How do these various sources of knowledge relate to the five-fold categorization of the standard account?

*Testimony*

When Basil refers to tradition he does so in a broad and a narrow sense. Broadly, he means beliefs of long-standing as opposed to innovation and he lauds those "whose soundness of character leads them to hold the dignity of antiquity to be more honourable than mere new-fangled novelty." (§16) Basil's opponents clearly share this view for their charge against Basil is precisely that of innovation. (§13) Basil regards this as serious and defends his fidelity to the tradition (see particularly §§71-75). In so doing he turns the accusation back upon his opponents: "The one aim of the whole band of opponents and enemies of 'sound doctrine' is to shake down the foundation of the faith of Christ by levelling apostolic tradition with the ground, and utterly destroying it." (§25)

Yet Basil also speaks of tradition in a narrower sense, in particular, he speaks of specific written and unwritten traditions:

---

[11] Hogg, "Knowledge of God," 108–14.

[12] See particularly William P. Alston, *Perceiving God: The Epistemology of Religious Experience* (Ithaca, NY: Cornell University Press, 1991).

> Of the beliefs and practices whether generally accepted or publicly enjoined which are preserved in the Church some we possess derived from written teaching; others we have received delivered to us "in a mystery" by the tradition of the apostles; and both of these in relation to true religion have the same force. (§66)

Through §66 and §67 Basil provides numerous examples of such traditions and the discussion is illuminating. Of particular interest is Basil's explanation as to why so many important beliefs and practices were never committed to writing. Simply put, they are too important to be the subject of public critique with its attendant risk of diminishing the "awful dignity of the mysteries" (§67):

> This is the reason for our tradition of unwritten precepts and practices, that the knowledge of our dogmas may not become neglected and contemned by the multitude through familiarity. "Dogma" and "Kerugma" are two distinct things; the former is observed in silence; the latter is proclaimed to all the world. (§67)

Although written and unwritten tradition are distinct, Basil states that the Fathers "followed the sense of Scripture, and started from the evidence which, a few sentences back, I deduced from Scripture and laid before you." (§16) Note here that Basil is defending the unwritten tradition, the use of "with" in the doxology, and this leads to some inconsistency. Is "with" to be regarded as "dogma" (written tradition) or "kerugma" (unwritten tradition)? Inconsistency aside, Basil's major point is that the two forms of tradition stand in harmony and together inform the proper bounds of Christian belief and practice.

Also important is the testimony of Christian authors such as Irenaeus, Clement of Rome, Dionysius of Rome and so on, to whom Basil appeals in defence of his fidelity to tradition (§§71-75). To them we might add Basil (and "others," §79) through whom the knowledge of God can come. We might, to employ Basil's own imagery, regard all such persons as "masters" to the "apprentices" in Christian faith.

Testimony, then, is a key source of knowledge for Basil. Often the term "testimony" is associated with the formal setting of the courtroom. Yet such formal testimony is neither the most frequent nor the most important kind. Informal testimony, which we might define simply as somebody's say-so that such-and-such is the case, is a pervasive, fundamental, and critical part of our intellectual landscape. "We do not even learn to speak or think without the help of others, and much of what we know depends upon what they tell us."[13] Such dependence is found even in highly developed theoretical matters including the sciences[14] and mathematics.[15] There are many significant issues which arise in respect of testimony as a source of knowledge. It is certain, however, that Basil thinks the testimony of the apostles and fathers ought to inform Christian belief and practice. More, he regards them as sources of the knowledge of God.

*Holy Spirit*

We have seen already that Basil regards the Holy Spirit as acting in some epistemic capacity: "The way of the knowledge of God lies from One Spirit through the One Son to the One Father." (§47) Later I will discuss the nuances of Basil's view on how the Spirit works as an epistemic agent. For now the question is simply whether Basil regards the Holy Spirit as a source for the knowledge of God and, if so, how this source relates to the five categories provided by the standard account: perception, reason, introspection, memory, and testimony.

Of these we may immediately by-pass three—reason, introspection, and memory—for none of these parallel the sort of epistemic work Basil ascribes to the Holy Spirit. This leaves us with testimony and perception as the categories under which Basil's understanding of the work of the Holy Spirit may be subsumed. Now, it is a peculiarity of testimony that it depends upon perception—one must hear (or otherwise perceive) testimony. Thus, if the Holy Spirit does indeed "testify" then this actually requires perception of the Holy Spirit (or something like it) by some person at some time. So when Basil introduces citations from scripture with phrases such as "the Holy Spirit bears witness that" (§15) and "it is the Spirit which says" (§49) it implies that the Holy Spirit was "perceived" at some prior time and is, therefore, perceivable. This is not simply to say that the reader of scripture "perceives" the Spirit speaking through scripture, but that the original authors of scripture somehow "perceived" what they later recorded. It is "inspiration" of the author, not "illumination" of the reader which I have in view here.

*DSS* does not limit the epistemic role of the Holy Spirit to some prior time, however. Rather, the Spirit plays a role in the enlightenment of present day believers. Thus:

---

[13] Audi, *Epistemology*, 130.

[14] C.A.J. Coady, *Testimony: A Philosophical Study* (Oxford: Clarendon Press, 1992), 8–11.

[15] Audi, *Epistemology*, 249–61.

> ...when, by means of the power that enlightens us, we fix our eyes on the beauty of the image of the invisible God, and through the image are led up to the supreme beauty of the spectacle of the archetype, then, I ween, is with us inseparably the Spirit of knowledge, in Himself bestowing on them that love the vision of the truth the power of beholding the Image, not making the exhibition from without, but in Himself leading on to the full knowledge. (§47)

Here not only do we see that Basil regards the Spirit as acting in the present, but acting in a mode analogous to sight. The same analogy reoccurs later:

> ...as is the power of seeing in the healthy eye, so is the operation of the Spirit in the purified soul. Wherefore also Paul prays for the Ephesians that they may have their 'eyes enlightened' by 'the Spirit of wisdom.'" (§61)

I will have more to say on the epistemic role of the Holy Spirit below. For now we may conclude simply that Basil regards "spiritual perception" as one of the sources of our knowledge of God.

There is next to no appeal to reason, introspection, and memory as sources of the knowledge of God in *DSS*. Basil does seek to argue "rationally" but reason as a method is not the same as reason as a source of knowledge. In any case, Basil is concerned to demonstrate his fidelity to tradition—a purpose which would be undermined by appeal to philosophical arguments. Actually, Basil thinks his opponents have departed from tradition precisely because of "their close study of heathen writers" (§5) and *DSS* is pervaded with an obvious antipathy toward "vain philosophy" (§5), "unpractical philosophy and vain delusion" (§5), "the pettiness of Paganism" (§6), and so on. Neither does introspection find any place. Introspection should not be confused with "the inward witness of the Spirit" which ought correctly to be taken as a form of perception. The same distinction is found in Rudolf Otto's critique of Schleiermacher's "feeling of absolute dependence," which speaks only to the state of mind of the believer as opposed to something outside the self (i.e. God).[16] As for memory, although our recollection always plays an important part in knowing, Basil's comments on that topic are exhausted by a critical remark in

---

[16] Rudolf Otto, *The Idea of the Holy: An Inquiry into the Non-Rational Factor in the Idea of the Divine and Its Relation to the Rational*, trans. John W. Harvey, Revised with additions (London: Oxford University Press, 1936), 10.

regards of those who don't remember the teachings of scripture (§15) and a citation of John 16:13 ("the Comforter...will put you in remembrance," §49). Ultimately, it is testimony (via scripture and tradition) and perception (of the Holy Spirit) which are the most interesting sources of knowledge in *DSS*.

## The Structure of Knowledge

Having considered the sources of knowledge in *DSS*, the next question pertains to how such sources are used. This is the question of the structure of knowledge. Given that *DSS* focuses mainly upon testimony and perception (of the Spirit) the major interest lies in how these two important sources of knowledge fit together. I begin with the observation that Basil's use of scripture and tradition is relatively simple in as much as he clearly believes that citing such testimony is tantamount to demonstrating the truth of the claim in question. The more complicated, hence interesting, question is how the Holy Spirit is understood to play a role in the formation of knowledge.

## The Role of the Spirit, Religious Experience and Belief Formation

An analysis of the epistemic role of the Holy Spirit in *DSS* will be aided by understanding the different ways in which religious experience relates to belief formation. William P. Alston discusses three ways in which this may occur.[17] First, some experiences may not be experiences of God, but are nevertheless well explained by appeal to divine activity. Perhaps one prays for, and then experiences, the ability to forgive a person who has caused great personal offence. One may thereby be justified in holding that God granted such ability. Second, one might, through the medium of some other activity, feel that God is present such that one "sees" that God is there. Here one is aware not merely of the presence of God, but that God is present "in" or "through" some other experience: listening to Handel's Messiah, or watching a sunset, or some-such. Such a mediated experience we may regard as involving indirect perception of God. Third, one may feel that God is present but not "in" or "through" any other experience and such an unmediated experience we may regard as a direct perception of God.

---

[17] Alston, *Perceiving God*, 286–88.

These three modes of belief formation vary in the immediacy with which God is taken to be present, with a direct perception of God being most immediate and invoking God as explanation the least immediate. It is possible for God to less immediate again as in the case where an experience is enjoyed by one person who then forms a religious belief which is accepted by a second person on the basis of the first person's testimony.

We thus have four ways in which religious experience may give rise to belief formation:

1. A person forms a belief based on the testimony of others.
2. A person has an experience which is best explained by a religious belief.
3. A person formulates a religious belief as a result of a mediated experience of God.
4. A person formulates a religious belief as a result of an unmediated experience of God.

Now, note that such modes are not exclusive. One could, for instance, form the belief that God is loving on the basis of a reading of scripture (say John 3:16), or because one experienced an event for which "God is loving" is taken to be the best explanation, or because one experienced the love of God through the kindness of a friend, or because one apprehended the love of God directly. The various modes could then become mutually supporting or confirmatory in the process of forming the belief "God is loving." We should be aware, then, that we might find one or all of these modes of belief formation expressed in *DSS*.

*DSS* holds that there is no knowledge of God apart from the work of the Holy Spirit. It is worth noting here that Basil regards the operations of the Spirit as so extensive (cf. §23, §39, §49, §56) that the danger is always to understate the Spirit's importance (§49) and, this being the case, it is likely impossible to overstate the importance of the Spirit's epistemic agency. To turn to specific claims, the knowledge of God can come only "by the Spirit" (§27) for revelation of mysteries is "the peculiar function of the Spirit" (§38). In a detailed discussion (§47) we find that the Spirit enlightens, enabling us to see "the image of the invisible God," and leading us on to "the full knowledge." Here (cf. also §27) Basil cites Matthew 11:27 ("No one knows the Father except by the Son") in conjunction with 1 Corinthians 12:3 ("no one can say Jesus is Lord accept by the Holy Spirit") on his way to the Trinitarian affirmation: "the way of the knowledge of God lies from One Spirit through the One Son to the One Father." The epistemic argument here is directly dependent upon the divinity of the Spirit for "in Himself He shows the glory of the Only begotten, and on true worshippers He in Himself bestows the knowledge of God." A similar idea occurs earlier: "He, like the sun, will by the aid of thy purified eye show thee in Himself the image of the invisible, and in the blessed spectacle of the image thou shalt behold the unspeakable beauty of the archetype." (§23) It is precisely because the Spirit shares the divine nature that he "knoweth the things of God, as 'the spirit of man that is in him.'" (§50 cf. §40) Having such knowledge "in himself", the Spirit is able to impart it to others not as a mere messenger, but as God himself. Similar thoughts are expressed in §64.

The foregoing provides a fair *prima facie* case for thinking that the proclamations of scripture must find their genesis in the revelatory action of the Spirit. This is confirmed when Basil introduces citations from scripture with "it is the Spirit which says, as the Lord says" (§49) showing not just that we hear the voice of the Spirit in scripture, but that this voice is the voice of God himself. The deity of the Spirit is, again, intimately connected with his capacity as the revealer of divine mysteries. For present purposes the important point is that *DSS* affirms the first mode of belief formation in which a person may form a belief based on the testimony of others, here the authors of scripture, as to their own religious experiences.

It is clear, however, that all that has just been said about the central epistemic role of the Spirit applies to all those who come to faith. If scripture records that knowledge came to previous generations through the action of the Spirit, such epistemic agency is also required if this knowledge is to be appropriated by later readers. This is the third mode of belief formation in which knowledge comes "through" a mediated experience, in this case the experience of reading scripture.

There is more to be said about this idea of "knowing through," however, as there are other channels besides that of scripture. There is that other channel of testimony, unwritten tradition, by which people may come to the knowledge of God. Basil three times speaks of the knowledge of God in the context of a discussion on baptism (§26, 35, 75). Indeed, he seems to suggest that baptism is the beginning of the knowledge of God, a somewhat curious view if one takes baptism as something one does subsequent to a confession of faith. What interests Basil in these passages on baptism, however, is not the place of faith, but the Triune baptismal confession. As confession of "Father, Son, and Holy Spirit" in baptism is such a central aspect of Christian tradition, Basil enlists it as evidence both of the full equality of the Spirit and his own fidelity to tradition. Importantly, however, the confession is itself a source of knowledge for through it "He gave us the boon of the knowledge of the faith which leads to salvation, by means of holy names." (§44) The mention of "holy names" is an allusion to the idea that "names" (and here "Father," "Son," and "Holy Spirit" count as such) can give us some knowledge of that to which they refer.[18] This is a complex issue and I will not explore it here. Suffice to say, Basil believes that knowledge can come through Christian tradition, particularly the Triune formula used in baptism.

There is one more instance of "knowing through": *DSS* itself. At the outset Basil invokes "the help...of the Holy Spirit Himself" (§2) whilst he concludes with the assurance that "either through me or through others the Lord will grant full explanation on matters which have yet to be made clear, according to the knowledge supplied to the worthy by the Holy Spirit." (§79). As in the case of scripture, Basil sees that both author and reader will need the aid of the Spirit if *DSS* is to contribute to a knowledge of God. Doubtlessly the same would apply to any spoken communication, such as preaching. It is important, however, to note that the "Spirit of truth" (§22) could hardly be expected to lend authority to a lie. So whilst the tradition can be presented in innovative ways, ultimately all claims must be consistent with tradition if the Spirit is to affirm their truth. With this in mind, it is clear that *DSS* presents the idea that a person can form a religious belief "through" the tradition howsoever that tradition might be expressed.

What of the two remaining modes of belief formation enumerated above? That beliefs can be formed in order to explain an experience occurs but is not prevalent. In §39, for instance, Basil speaks of "the dispensations made for man" and asks "who will gainsay their having been accomplished through the grace of the Spirit?" He has in mind such "ancient evidence" as "valorous feats in war" and "signs wrought through just men," and Basil essentially invites us to

---

[18] David G. Robertson, "A Patristic Theory of Proper Names," *Archiv Für Geschichte Der Philosophie* 84, no. 1 (January 14, 2002): 1–19, doi:10.1515/agph.2002.002, provides a helpful discussion.

see the action of the Spirit as the best explanation of the evidence. As respects the formation of beliefs as a result of an unmediated experience of God, Basil has little to say. This is not surprising given that Basil is defending himself from a charge of innovation. To appeal to unmediated religious experience, which is by definition an intensely personal source of belief, would hardly help to answer such a charge.

We may conclude, then, that of the four modes of belief formation initially considered all except belief formation on the basis of unmediated religious experience find some place in *DSS*.

**Epistemic Reductionism**

One significant question which can be put to any set of claims about knowledge is whether or not they are reducible. Here the idea is that knowledge claims of one sort are justified when they are "reduced" to knowledge claims of another sort. A good example of reductionism is found in common treatments of testimony where it is often held that people's say-so is generally sufficiently unreliable that one should not accept it without support from other sources.[19] Space precludes a detailed investigation of such question in respects of *DSS*, but a cursory examination suggests that Basil does not generally view the knowledge of God in reductionist terms.

We have seen that Basil places great emphasis upon testimony in the form of written or unwritten tradition. Now to greatly simplify the issue, reductionist theories of testimony tend to emphasis the unreliability of testimony, whilst non-reductionist theories tend to emphasise its reliability. It should be apparent that Basil takes the reliability of the tradition for granted and takes it that theological truth claims can be justified solely by appeal to it. There are no grounds for thinking Basil would understand the testimony of the tradition in reductionist terms.

Nor does Basil regard the epistemic work done by the Holy Spirit as needing justification from other sources. Given the fundamental importance of the Spirit's epistemic role there could, in any case, be nothing more fundamental to which one could appeal by way of justification. Ultimately there is no other source for a knowledge of God than God himself, a point succinctly made when Basil's

---

[19] For a detailed treatment of such themes see Sanford C. Goldberg, "Reductionism and the Distinctiveness of Testimonial Knowledge," in *The Epistemology of Testimony*, ed. Jennifer Lackey and Ernest Sosa (Oxford: Clarendon Press, 2006), 127–44.

appeals to 1 Corinthians 2:11: "the things of God knoweth no man but the Spirit of God." (§40)

A tension arises in consequence of the foregoing remarks. If the epistemic work of the Holy Spirit is fundamental, how is it that the tradition is itself not reducible? The key is to understand that testimony is not a generative source of knowledge but a means of transmitting knowledge derived from other sources. To say that testimony is not reductionist is not to deny this ultimate dependence, it is merely to say that the recipient of testimony does not need to go back to this initial source. So if, for example, a person claims to have seen John at a party last night we can recognise that this claim is ultimately dependent upon the person having seen John at the party without needing to "see for ourselves." As it turns out, Basil does think that the claims of scripture are affirmed by the witness of the Spirit, but this is a different thing from saying that we are unjustified in accepting the claims of scripture as they stand.

**Epistemic Holism and Coherentism**

If the various forms of knowledge discussed in *DSS* are irreducible, then this leaves the question of how they are related. The answer is a relatively simple one: *DSS* propounds a version of holism. The idea here is that the same belief might arise from, and be justified on, a number of independent grounds. This is an idea already touched upon in the previous remarks on belief formation. There it was suggested that the belief "God is loving" could arise in various independent ways. Contrast this with foundationalism, the idea that there are a few foundational beliefs which need no justification but which serve to justify all other beliefs in our edifice of knowledge. Here the philosophical project of Descartes is the paradigm case. However *DSS* is more epistemically generous, so to speak. It holds that beliefs may be justified by appeal to either written or unwritten tradition, and that there are various modes of belief formation which obtain justification through their coherence with other beliefs. Here think in terms of a "web of beliefs" in which "a person's belief is justified when it fits together with the person's other beliefs in a coherent way."[20] In such a view what matters is that a belief finds agreement with the system of belief of which it is a part. A claim such as "God is loving" does not, in such a schema,

---

[20] Feldman, *Epistemology*, 51.

find justification because it is derived from a small set of foundational beliefs, but because it arises from multiple independent sources and coheres with other, similarly independent, beliefs.

**Virtue Epistemology**

Basil presents what may be regarded as a Virtue Epistemology. This is an approach to knowledge which was popular in the patristic period and takes "intellectual agents and communities [as] the primary source of epistemic value and the primary focus of epistemic evaluation."[21] Such an approach lays emphasis upon intellectual (or doxastic) virtues such as "wisdom, prudence, foresight, understanding, discernment, truthfulness and studiousness, among others."[22] The opposing vices include "folly, obtuseness, gullibility, dishonesty, willful naiveté and vicious curiosity to name a few."[23] Wood remarks that:

> the pursuit of intellectual virtue, while presently unfashionable, was the dominant way of casting epistemological concerns in the writings of Aristotle, Augustine, Thomas Aquinas and other philosophers of the ancient and medieval tradition. Your intellectual life is important, according to these thinkers, for the simple reason that your very character, the kind of person you are and are becoming, is at stake.[24]

Such an approach may be contrasted with non-virtue approaches which, crudely put, abstract the knower out of the process of knowing and which therefore hold that issues of character are of no moment in the formation of knowledge.

It is clear upon reading Basil that he places tremendous emphasis upon the intellectual virtues and that his position accords exactly with the idea that "your very character, the kind of person you are and are becoming, is at stake." Basil regards our knowledge of God as dependent upon the exercise of intellectual virtue and the eschewal of intellectual vice.

That Basil approves of intellectual virtue is very clear when one considers his introductory remarks. In §1 Amphilocus is ("highly")

---

[21] John Greco and John Turri, "Virtue Epistemology," ed. Edward N. Zalta, *Stanford Encyclopedia of Philosophy*, 2009, http://plato.stanford.edu/archives/spr2010/entries/epistemology-virtue/.

[22] W. Jay Wood, *Epistemology: Becoming Intellectually Virtuous*, Contours of Christian Philosophy (Downers Grove, IL: InterVarsity Press, 1998), 16.

[23] Ibid.

[24] Ibid., 16–17.

commended for his "desire for information" and "industrious energy," "care and watchfulness," "diligence in asking," "honest desire to arrive at the actual truth," and for possessing "a character desirous of information, and seeking the truth as a remedy for ignorance." Amphilochus' awareness of the subtleties of theological reflection are noted: "shewn in the expression of your opinion that of all the terms concerning God in every mode of speech, not one ought to be left without exact investigation" and Basil suggests that this is an outworking of the reading of scripture on Amphilochius' part: "You have turned to good account your reading of the exhortation of the Lord."

Basil also commends Amphilochius' character in the closing section. Here Basil recounts his motives in writing which include not only his love for Amphilochius and sense of duty (§79), but also by his assurance of Amphilochius' good character.

> A further powerful incentive to my undertaking was the warm fervour of your "love unfeigned," and the seriousness and taciturnity of your disposition; a guarantee that you would not publish what I was about to say to all the world,—not because it would not be worth making known, but to avoid casting pearls before swine. (§79)

Ironically, the fact *DSS* is in our possession might be taken to show that Basil's reliance upon Amphilochius' discretion was here misplaced. But this should not distract us from an important point: namely, that *DSS* was in the first instance private correspondence not intended to be cast "before swine." Clearly Basil intended his comments should be directed only where the good character (as he supposed) of the recipient could ensure a positive reception.

A few further remarks scattered through the work conform this was indeed Basil's attitude. Basil cites numerous passages which "the diligent reader" (§9) will see support Basil's contention. Here much reliance is placed upon the reader and Basil trusts so much in Amphilochius' diligence that he feels at liberty to enumerate only a portion of the scriptural evidence:

> We have only touched cursorily on these proofs, because our object is to pass on to other points. You at your leisure can put together the items of the evidence, and then contemplate the height of the glory and the preeminence of the power of the Only Begotten. (§15)

In the same place Basil goes on to refer to "the well-disposed hearer" and whilst he here has in mind the "hearer" of Christian scripture, he later applies the same sort of idea to his own writing:

"Kindly readers will find a satisfactory defence in what I have said." (§75)

Even the presence and work of the Holy Spirit is connected to the merit of an individual for the Spirit distributes gifts "according to each recipient's worth" (§37) and "dwells in those that are worthy." (§63) The grace flowing from the Spirit ebbs and flows like heat in iron "even if on account of the firmness of the recipients' disposition to good the grace abides with them continually." (§63) Most tellingly "we render thanks to our God for the benefits we have received, according to the measure of our purification from evil, as we receive one a larger and another a smaller share of the aid of the Spirit." (§63)

There is, of course, a converse to all of this and just as Basil commends intellectual virtue he condemns intellectual vice. He speaks, for instance, of:

> ...captious listeners and questioners...who advance arguments, not so much with the view of getting any good out of them, as in order that, in the event of their failing to elicit answers which chime in with their own desires, they may seem to have fair ground for controversy. (§1)

Whilst there certainly is a polemical edge to this such that sometimes Basil's criticisms amount to little more than name-calling,[25] it is clear that he does indeed regard certain habits of mind as hindering an increase in knowledge. Such habits of mind are, of course, the converse of the intellectual virtues already discussed.

## Conclusion

We have seen that knowledge plays a central part in *DSS*. Knowledge is important for Basil because upon it depends the believer's transformation into the likeness of God. Such knowledge is multi-faceted and involves propositional, tacit, and relational forms of knowing. These are largely independent but still inter-related. There are two primary sources for the knowledge of God—tradition and the Spirit—and these too are inter-related. Indeed, "independent but inter-related" is a characteristic feature of Basil's multi-faceted epistemology and leads us to regard his epistemology as a form of holism. There is, for Basil, no foundational claim or

---

[25] Consider here the parallels with Basil's *Contra Eunomius*. See Basil of Caesarea, *Against Eunomius*, trans. Mark DelCogliano and Andrew Radde-Gallwitz, The Fathers of the Church: A New Translation 122 (Washington, DC: Catholic University of America Press, 2011), 38–45.

claims to which one might appeal in order to justify the whole of our knowledge of God.

A major element of Basil's epistemology is his understanding of the roles of epistemic virtue and epistemic vice. In adopting a form of virtue epistemology, it is clear that Basil ties knowing to character and, as knowing is also tied to salvation, so a person's character takes on soteriological significance.

A number of important consequences flow from this. First, we see that Trinitarian theology is hardly superfluous to Christian living. Indeed, it is no stretch to conclude from a reading of *DSS* that Christian discipleship is shaped in no small part by the Trinitarian nature of God. In particular, there should be great emphasis upon the Spirit and his works including, but not limited to, his epistemic agency. Ultimately, the Christian knowledge of God is a spiritual knowledge which encompasses the entire person.

Second, we see that many contemporary discussions of epistemology are, from the perspective of Christian theology, largely misguided. Contrary to many epistemological schemas not all knowledge is reducible to one sort. Neither rationalism nor empiricism, the two great categories of epistemological discussion, are adequate to account for the sort of knowledge which Basil asserts is possible. In addition, Christian theology, at least in as much as it is concerned with justifying Christian truth claims, ought to look more to coherentist than foundationalist accounts of justification.

Third, in respect of the sources of knowledge care should be taken not to overemphasise the role of scripture. To be sure, Basil thinks that Christian beliefs ought to be consistent with scripture, but when we start to see scripture as the primary source of knowledge, so marginalising both the Spirit and the broader Christian tradition, we risk falling into a narrow rationalism which hardly does justice to Christian knowledge as Basil portrays it.

Fourth, the focus upon virtue epistemology is important in as much as it reminds us that habits of mind matter. All too often Christian theology is discussed in ways which are lacking in Christian charity. Basil reminds us that such attitudes can actually hinder our growth in knowledge and therefore risk that very transformation into the likeness of God which is the ultimate end of Christian faith.

Such are some of the consequences which flow from this all too brief consideration of Basil's extraordinarily rich treatment of the nature and role of the Spirit.

# God as Husband and Jesus as Bridegroom: A Critical Reassessment of the Divine Conjugal Metaphor

Gillian Asquith

Melbourne School of Theology

Abstract

*The prohibition against a man remarrying a woman whom he had previously divorced (Deut 24:1-4) supplies the hermeneutical lens for the OT metaphor of God as husband. When God's promises to restore his covenant people in relationship with himself are interpreted in light of this prohibition, the divine conjugal metaphor becomes a powerful representation of God's unprecedented forgiveness. This expression of God's grace lies behind the NT development of the metaphor. The OT envisaged God as Israel's future husband, but the gospels use the metaphor christologically to place Jesus within the identity of the eschatological bridegroom. Matthew's parables introduce judgement into the metaphor and redefine the new covenant community. The Pauline corpus and Revelation draw heavily upon the metaphor's OT background such that the final consummation of the relationship between Christ and the church constitutes the ultimate fulfilment of grace and forgiveness shown by the God of second chances to a sinful people.*

## Introduction

The concepts of love and romance hold enormous appeal, and a quick glance at the magazine stand in any newsagency confirms the amount of popular interest in finding new romance, rekindling stale romance, experiencing vicarious romance or ruing broken romance. Popular Christian literature is no different, and all the above aspects of love and romance are represented in parenetic and fictional Christian works. Moreover, it is not uncommon to find Christian literature that presents salvation history as a divine romance and exhorts the individual believer to pursue an intimate relationship with God in marital terms, appealing to the divine conjugal metaphor of God as husband and Christ as bridegroom for its biblical warrant.[1] However, this paper contends that filling divine conjugal imagery with the Western, individualistic notion of marriage as the union of two people based on romantic love and intended for individual fulfilment, mutual support and complementary companionship creates a distorted interpretation of the marriage metaphor's intent.

Hosea, Isaiah, Ezekiel and Jeremiah present Israel as God's metaphorical wife although she is far from a model of marital fidelity. She has violated her relationship with God through illicit liaisons with foreign gods and foreign powers. Despite her unfaithfulness and the rupture of the metaphorical marriage, God promises that he will restore Israel in a new, eschatological, nuptial relationship with himself. In the NT, that bridegroom is Jesus and the relationship between God and his people is restored in the descent of the New Jerusalem from heaven as a bride, the metaphorical wife of the Lamb (Rev 21:9-10).

A number of scholars assume that the development of the marriage metaphor in the OT proves the essentially marital relationship between God and Israel.[2] Claude Chavasse credits Hosea with having brought 'into consciousness the essentially nuptial character of the nexus between Yahweh and Israel.'[3] Raymond C. Ortlund maintains that his exegetical explorations 'open up the nexus of meanings informed by the idea that the bond between Yahweh and Israel is marital in nature.'[4] Nelly Stienstra bases her discussion of YHWH as the husband of his people on the premise that the covenant on Mount Sinai was YHWH's marriage with his people.[5]

Despite points of correspondence between marriage and Israel's covenant relationship with God, close examination of the divine

---

[1] See, for example, Dee Brestin & Kathy Troccoli, *Falling in Love with Jesus: Abandoning Yourself to the Greatest Romance of Your Life* (Nashville, TN: W Publishing, 2000) or Alan D. Wright, *Lover of my Soul: Delighting in God's Passionate Love* (Sisters, OR: Multnomah, 1998).

[2] The nature of the relationship between the prophetic writings and the Pentateuch is somewhat problematic when determining the development of the divine conjugal metaphor, but happily, the salient features of the marriage metaphor are not materially affected by diachronic considerations.

[3] Claude Chavasse, *The Bride of Christ: An Enquiry into the Nuptial Element in Early Christianity* (London: Faber and Faber, 1940), 28.

[4] Raymond C. Ortlund Jr., *God's Unfaithful Wife: A Biblical Theology of Spiritual Adultery* (New Studies in Biblical Theology 2; Leicester: Apollos, 1996), 26.

[5] Nelly Stienstra, *YHWH is the Husband of His People: Analysis of a Biblical Metaphor with Special Reference to Translation* (Kampen: Kok Pharos, 1993), 134, 184.

conjugal metaphor suggests that its primary function was not to demonstrate an essentially marital nature to that relationship. Rather, it served as a powerful representation of God's unprecedented forgiveness in response to his people's unfaithfulness. The distinction is subtle but important, and underpins a thematic unity to the metaphor in the Old Testament and its development in the New.[6] In the OT, the covenantal basis of marriage as an exclusive relationship allowed the metaphor to express Israel's covenant infidelity and God's incomparable covenant faithfulness and grace in a unique way. In the NT, the metaphor was subject to both continuity and development as Christ was identified as the eschatological bridegroom of the church. However, even when applied to Christ, the metaphor served as far more than an expression of his intimate relationship with the church.

**Marriage as a Covenant**

Marriage is an especially appropriate metaphor for the covenant relationship between God and his people because marriage itself is a covenant.[7] The biblical concept of covenant is rooted in ANE international treaty formularies which defined vassal relationships between kings and their vanquished foes. These included a summary statement of the vassal's prescribed loyalty, and stipulations which ensured the exclusivity of the vassal's relationship with her suzerain. Covenant relationships provided for the security and protection of the subordinate party and carried sanctions against the breaking of their terms.[8]

In accordance with these covenantal criteria, Israel was commanded to דבק 'cleave to' God (Deut 10:20; 11:22; 13:4; 30:20; Josh 22:5; 23:8). The exclusivity of the covenant relationship was

---

[6] This is hinted at but not developed by Seock-Tae Sohn (*YHWH, the Husband of Israel: The Metaphor of Marriage between YHWH and Israel* (Eugene: Wipf & Stock, 2002), 143).

[7] There are no texts, biblical or extra-biblical, which identify marriage explicitly as a covenant. Although Ezek 16:8, Prov 2:17, and Mal 2:14 imply the covenantal nature of marriage, it could be argued that the referent for 'covenant' is the relationship between God and Israel as defined by the Sinaitic covenant. However, Gordon Paul Hugenberger demonstrates persuasively that when 'covenant' is defined as 'an elected, as opposed to natural, relationship of obligation under oath,' then marriage fulfils all the criteria necessary to its designation as a covenant (*Marriage as a Covenant: A Study of Biblical Law and Ethics Governing Marriage Developed from the Perspective of Malachi* (Leiden: Brill, 1994), 11).

[8] See Klaus Baltzer, *The Covenant Formulary in Old Testament, Jewish and Early Christian Writings* (tr. David E. Green; Oxford: Blackwell, 1971).

made explicit in the Decalogue when God's jealousy was linked with the prohibition against worshipping other gods (Exod 20:3-5). God's security and protection was one of the blessings of the covenant relationship such that Israel would receive rest from her enemies and live in safety in the land (Deut 12:10).

Likewise, the marriage bond was to be one of permanent loyalty to the exclusion of all others. In the Genesis narrative of the paradigmatic first marriage, a man 'clings to his wife' (Gen 2:24), the verb דבק ('unite, cleave or cling to') carrying the connotation of permanently sticking to someone or something. Marriage provided security and protection for the subordinate party, a feature highlighted by Naomi's desire for her daughters-in-law to find מנוחה ('security') with a husband (Ruth 1:8-9). Marriage, too, was protected by legal sanctions ranging from the payment of a fine for sex with an unattached girl of marriageable age (Deut 22:29) to the death penalty for adultery (Lev 20:10; Deut 22:22).

The sanctity of marriage in ancient Israel, however, extended beyond its covenantal nature. Israel's relationship with God lent a peculiarly theological significance to marriage and transgressions against it within the Israelite community. As God's covenant partner, Israel was a people defined by obedience.[9] The nexus of God's unconditional election of Israel with the reciprocal obligation to obedience was the land. It was known as Israel's inheritance and the familial property rights generated by this inheritance were symbolic of belonging within the covenant community. That portion of land 'owned' by a household was the locus of each individual's participation in the privileges and protection afforded by being the people of God.[10] Therefore, the family on its inherited landholding was the vehicle for the bilateral expression of the covenant relationship between Israel and God. Anything which threatened a household's capacity for continued existence on its patrimonial landholding, including rupture of the integrity of marriage, struck at the very heart of the covenant relationship and in turn threatened Israel's continued enjoyment of the land (Deut 4:40).[11]

---

[9] Walter Brueggemann, *Theology of the Old Testament: Testimony, Dispute, Advocacy* (Minneapolis: Fortress, 1997), 417.

[10] Christopher J. H. Wright, *God's People in God's Land: Family, Land and Property in the Old Testament* (Grand Rapids: Eerdmans, 1990), 88.

[11] Wright, *God's People*, 207.

Therefore, the theological significance of the exclusivity of marriage was such that any violation of the marriage relationship correspondingly violated the covenant relationship between Israel and God. The covenantal nature of marriage and the theological significance of its exclusivity rendered marital infidelity a profoundly effective vehicle for expressing both Israel's covenant infidelity and God's incomparable covenant faithfulness and grace.

## The Divine Conjugal Metaphor in the Old Testament

The dominant use of the conjugal metaphor in the OT describes Israel as God's wife, and more particularly, as God's unfaithful wife. Her status as wife, of course, presumes God's role as husband. However, the concept of God as Israel's husband is left almost entirely undeveloped across the OT. It is striking that all the texts that speak of God as husband do so in contexts either contrasting Israel's flagrant unfaithfulness in the present with the past, or describing God's intentions to restore his relationship with her in the future. Imagery of Israel enjoying a current, functional, intimate, marital relationship with God is absent. Accordingly, instances of the metaphor of God as Israel's husband fall into three categories which provide a helpful framework for examining the conjugal metaphor in Hosea, Isaiah, Jeremiah and Ezekiel:

- a) God describes himself as Israel's husband in retrospect; conjugal imagery is applied to God's relationship with Israel in the past in order to highlight current covenant infidelity.
- b) God describes himself as Israel's cuckolded husband.
- c) God describes himself as Israel's future husband; he intends to chastise Israel for her behaviour according to the cultural norm, but will ultimately restore her as his wife in an unprecedented contravention of accepted practice.

## Hosea

Hosea's sign-action, his marriage to 'a promiscuous wife' (Hos 1:2, HCSB), introduces the analogy of God as the husband of an unfaithful wife.[12] Hosea's message begins with a summarizing preface: the land is committing blatant acts of promiscuity by

---

[12] The precise status of Gomer as 'a wife of promiscuity' is debated but there is no doubt that Hosea's sign-act served to emphasise the repugnance of Israel's behaviour and cast God as the cuckolded husband.

abandoning the LORD (1:2); God's demand for exclusivity will override his inclination towards mercy; he will withdraw his compassion from Israel and reject her (1:4-6), and Judah will likewise be punished (1:9).

The broken marriage metaphor continues in terms reminiscent of a legal suit against Israel in which she stands accused of adultery (2:2-13).[13] Once again, God is the cuckolded husband, filing his case in language typical of the ANE divorce formula: 'she is not my wife and I am not her husband' (2:2). Israel has been unfaithful and committed adultery; she has gone after other lovers, attributing the material provisions lavished upon her by God to the Canaanite baals (2:5, 8) and violating the first commandment of the Decalogue.

God's role as husband and provider in the past is hinted at but not developed (2:7); Israel will acknowledge him as such only after he has deprived her of the prosperity that she has attributed to Baal. Hence the conjugal metaphor is not used to illuminate God's early relationship with Israel, but to emphasise how the contrast between Israel's pending punishment and the recollection of her previous relationship with God will rekindle her love for him.

In a surprising turn, God as cuckolded husband suddenly gives way to God as future husband (2:14-23). He will take the initiative to win Israel back by metaphorically returning her to the wilderness, the place where she trusted and followed him in her youth, relatively speaking at least (2:14-15). 'That day' (2:16) will herald an eschatological era of new relationship characterised by mutual intimacy: God will speak tenderly to Israel as he woos her back, and Israel, in turn, will address him by the term of endearment 'my husband' (אישי). 'My husband' suggests the existence of a deep personal relationship within marriage, over against בעלי '*ba'ali*, my lord' which, in a clever pun with Baal, emphasises the legal authority of a husband over his wife.[14]

The exclusivity of the covenant relationship will be restored as God removes the names of the baals from Israel's lips (2:17), and God's sovereign act of covenant renewal will result in an eternal

---

[13] The MT divides chs. 1 and 2 after 1:9. This study will follow the English division that begins ch. 2 after 1:11.

[14] Hans Walter Wolff, *Hosea: A Commentary on the Book of the Prophet Hosea* (tr. Gary Stansell; Hermeneia; Philadelphia: Fortress, 1974), 49.

relationship in which Israel's obedience is characterised by righteousness, justice, steadfast love, mercy and faithfulness (2:19-20). Israel's ability to respond to God with these attributes is only because God has contributed them first to the relationship.[15] In this way, Hosea anticipates the new covenant of Jer 31:31-34. Finally, in a reversal of Israel's 'forgetting' God (2:13), she will know (ידע) him (2:20). This verb of relational knowledge sums up the intimate communion and special association brought about as a result of the forgiveness of the unfaithful wife's adultery.

## Isaiah

Conjugal imagery in Isaiah focuses on the restoration of God's future relationship with his people. Isaiah 54 describes the wedding ceremony of Zion/Jerusalem (a synecdoche for Israel as a whole) to her king. The city's prior desolation is portrayed by a series of female experiences linked by the twin themes of shame and disgrace: infertility (Isa 54:1a), inability to marry (54:1c), and widowhood (54:4).

Yet God will redeem Jerusalem (54:5). The translation of the participle בעליך 'your husband' in most English versions reveals the translators' underlying assumption that the relationship between God and Israel is marital in nature. 'For your Maker is your husband' (NIV, NKJV, NRSV,) or vice versa (HCSB, NASB) suggests an ongoing marriage relationship. This is consonant with halakhic interpretation and the view adopted by a number of scholars that God had only divorced the Northern Kingdom; Judah was still married to him, leaving open the possibility for reconciliation.[16]

The rhetorical questions of Isa 50:1 provide the alleged textual basis for this: it is futile to look for Judah's divorce certificate because neither it, nor the creditors of 50:1b exist; Judah was neither divorced nor sold into slavery. However, this underplays the

---

[15] Francis I. Andersen and David Noel Freedman, *Hosea: A New Translation with Introduction and Commentary* (AB; New York: Doubleday, 1980), 283.

[16] See, for example, Baltzer, *Deutero-Isaiah*, 322; Joseph Blenkinsopp, *Isaiah 40-55* (AB; New York: Doubleday, 2002), 237; S. Borocin-Knol, 'Zion as an 'Agunah? An Interpretation of Isaiah 49:14; 50:1 and 54:6-8' in *"Enlarge the Site of Your Tent": The City as Unifying Theme in Isaiah*, (ed. Archibald L.H.M. van Wieringen; Oudtestamentische Studiën; Leiden: Brill, 2011), 191-206, esp. 203; David Instone-Brewer, *Divorce and Remarriage in the Bible: The Social and Literary Context* (Grand Rapids: Eerdmans, 2002), 49-50; J.A. Motyer, *The Prophecy of Isaiah* (Leicester: Inter-Varsity Press, 1993), 397; John D.W. Watts, *Isaiah 34-66* (rev.ed.; WBC; Nashville: Nelson, 2005), 798.

catastrophic effect of Judah's behaviour on her relationship with God and 50:1 is better understood as a rejection of the implied accusation that God had divorced Judah arbitrarily or that he had sold her because of a debt he owed. The LXX's ποῖον 'what kind of?' divorce certificate confirms that the question asks God's accusers to produce the certificate which shows the real reason for their mother's divorce: their sins. Thus בעליך is better translated verbally as 'the one who marries you' to convey the dynamic sense of the future wedding.[17]

In terms strikingly similar to Hos 2:19-20, God promises to restore his relationship with Zion with loving faithfulness and compassion (Isa 54:7-8). Instead of treating her like an adulterous woman whose repugnant behaviour justifies the penalty of a permanently terminated relationship, God vows to treat Zion like a wife who was abandoned through no fault of her own and deserves to be taken back (54:6). Interpretations which suggest that Zion was God's wife all along or which link the deserted and distressed wife of v.6 with the images of shame and reproach in v.4 miss the thrust of this declaration of unprecedented grace and forgiveness. In colloquial terms, Zion was the 'tart who deserved everything she got,' yet the comparative preposition כ 'as/like' indicates that she will be treated like an innocent young wife who was temporarily abandoned.

Isaiah does not present the restoration of God's relationship with Zion as a remarriage. Rather, it is more like a *new* marriage. The delight with which God will rejoice over Zion is likened to the rejoicing of a bridegroom over his bride (62:5). The importance attached to the sexual purity of a woman of marriageable age suggests that for God to delight over Zion as a bridegroom over his bride, she must be a virgin. The Song of Songs illustrates this kind of delight: the maiden is a locked garden and sealed fountain (4:12), the point of sexual union being the moment when 'her garden' (4:16) becomes 'his garden' (5:1). Likewise, Zion will become a locked garden and sealed fountain; the extent of God's forgiveness will remove all of her tainting from previous liaisons, and she will be made pure and virginal.

---

[17] Baltzer, *Deutero-Isaiah*, 422.

## Jeremiah

Jeremiah established the grounds for casting Judah as God's unfaithful wife by contrasting her current behaviour with the relationship between Israel and God in the past (Jer 2:2-3). As in Hosea, God is not specifically designated 'husband' here, but this role is implied by the description of Israel following him as a bride, and the wilderness years are presented as an idealised picture of Israel's obedience and loyalty. Like Hosea, Jeremiah uses the idealised portrayal of Israel's earlier relationship with God to emphasise the extent to which she has strayed from him (2:5), not to elaborate on God's role as her husband. Similarly, the statement that God was a husband to Israel at Jer 31:32 occurs in the context of emphasizing Israel's violation of the covenant.

Like Hosea, Jeremiah presents God as a cuckolded husband, publicly punishing Judah for her adulteries and shameless prostitution (13:26-27). God's retrospective indictment of the Northern Kingdom for adultery and his command to them to return emphasises his status as cuckold (3:6-14). The Hebrew reads:

שובו בנים שובבים נאם יהוה כי אנכי בעלתי

'Return, O turncoat children,' declares the LORD, 'for it is I who am your husband.'

(3:14, my translation)

Many English translations (for example, HCSB, NASB, NIV, NKJV, NRSV) imply that v.14 stands independently of the preceding strophe, the reason why Israel should return to God being because her relationship with him is marital: 'Return ... for I am your husband' (NIV).

However, the previous verse describes Israel's guilt and rebellion in sexual terms: 'you have scattered your favours among strangers under every green tree' (3:13). The emphatic first person pronoun אנכי indicates that these 'strangers' actually supply an antecedent referent for the causative כי 'for' clause; 'return ... for it is I who am your husband [as opposed to the foreign gods of v.13].' The reason why Israel should return is because it is God whom she should follow, not the foreign baals. It is God to whom she owes loyalty and commitment, even though she attributes his provision for her to idols of wood and stone (2:27). This coheres with the additional allegation that God's people have forgotten him (2:32) and that he is the spurned party in the relationship. Once again, the marriage metaphor and God's designation as husband emphasise the exclusivity of the covenant and Israel's unfaithful behaviour rather than an essentially marital nature to God's relationship with his people.

Thus far, Jeremiah's message is similar to Hosea's. However, Jeremiah makes explicit what Hosea and Isaiah leave unstated. Jeremiah asks whether a man should return to a woman who has left him and married another (3:1), since under Deuteronomic law, a man was prohibited from taking back a wife who had remarried after being divorced from her original husband (Deut 24:1-4). The expected answer, of course, is 'Absolutely not!' Employing *a fortiori* logic, this demonstrates that if a man could not take back his wife, then how much more impossible would it be for God to take back Israel?

Furthermore, Jeremiah implies that if the land is completely defiled when a man takes back a wife who had legitimately married a second husband, then how much more would it be defiled if he did so after she had taken illicit lovers (Jer 3:1b-2). Yet the unthinkable eventuates when God exhorts his people to return (3:14-18), announces that he will heal them of their backsliding and inability to repent, and promises to take them back (3:22). Thus conjugal imagery for Jeremiah is a rhetorical device to connect Israel's past, present and future,[18] and Jeremiah's hermeneutical premise highlights the extent of God's grace to an adulterous people who deserve the penalty of destruction.

## Ezekiel

Marital imagery is utilised to graphic effect in Ezekiel 16 and 23 for describing the wanton apostasy of God's covenant people. The marriage metaphor in Ezekiel, however, does not add anything of substantial theological import to this study that has not already been addressed. Restricting our discussion to Ezekiel 16, we will briefly point out the pertinent features of Ezekiel's deployment of the metaphor.

Ezekiel 16 is an extended metaphor, the rehearsal of God's previous saving acts serving as an incriminating background to his accusations. Ezekiel sets the context for Jerusalem's apostasy by retrospectively applying the role of husband to God (Ezek 16:8-14).

---

[18] Renita J. Weems, *Battered Love: Marriage, Sex, and Violence in the Hebrew Prophets* (Minneapolis: Fortress, 1995), 57.

God lavished affection upon his bride: he bathed her, clothed her with fine linen and adorned her with extravagant jewellery (16:9-14), but she scorned the ministrations of her husband and 'spread her legs' (16:25, NET) to every passer-by.

When God describes himself as Jerusalem's husband, it is in the context of her adultery and her preference for strangers over her own husband (16:32). Once again, the term 'husband' occurs in the context of 'cuckold.' Yet despite Jerusalem having despised his oath and broken the covenant, God will remember the covenant he made with her in happier days and establish an everlasting covenant instead (16:59-60). It is most likely that 'covenant' here is still a part of the extended conjugal metaphor and implicitly refers to the metaphorical marriage covenant.[19] Ezekiel's vulgar and explicit language depicts Jerusalem's behaviour in a most repulsive way, her excesses of depravity throwing into shocking relief the incomprehensible juxtaposition of culpability and restoration. Hence in Ezekiel, as in Hosea, Isaiah and Jeremiah, the conjugal metaphor emphasises the extent of God's grace in response to the most profligate displays of ingratitude and unfaithfulness.

It is striking that the elements of the divine conjugal metaphor appropriated by the prophets focus on the covenantal nature of marriage, the exclusivity of the relationship and the punishment due for its betrayal. The legal prohibition against a man remarrying a woman whom he had divorced but who had married a second husband supplies the interpretive key to the conjugal metaphor. Jeremiah briefly mentions the law of Deut 24:1-4, but the other prophets assume the audience's capacity for viewing the metaphor through this hermeneutical lens.

When the prohibition against remarrying a woman who had been sexually involved with another man is combined with Israel's theologico-cultural attitude towards marital infidelity — adultery was the vilest of sins and justified the harshest of punishments — then the conjugal metaphor becomes a powerful representation of God's grace and forgiveness. It is a portrayal of YHWH as the God of second chances, the God who blots out the transgressions of his people and remembers their sins no more (Isa 43:25). It is a metaphor that manages to combine the worst of humanity's sin with the overwhelming riches of God's grace, confronting and comforting at the same time.

---

[19] Hugenberger, *Marriage*, 308.

# The Divine Conjugal Metaphor in the New Testament

## The Gospels

The prophets had anticipated a time when God would heal his people of their backsliding and inability to repent (Jer 3:22), and betroth them in an unbreakable covenant with righteousness, justice, love, mercy and faithfulness (Hos 2:19-20). They invariably presented the eschatological bridegroom as God himself, never an agent such as the Isaianic Servant or Messiah. This is significant for the way in which the metaphor is appropriated and developed in the gospels and raises the question whether Jesus' messianic identity represented a shift in the person of the bridegroom from God to Messiah.

The Old Testament did not provide the first century CE with a clear messianic blueprint.[20] However, common elements of messianic expectation within the various strands of Second Temple Judaism included a preeminent agent of God (either human or heavenly), and a redeemer/royal figure in the tradition of King David who would deliver earthly Israel from its ongoing subjugation under foreign rule and inaugurate the eschatological age and reign of God.[21] 'Messianic' did not necessarily imply 'divine,' but as the Messiah was redefined in the light of Jesus' person and mission, so terms such as Messiah, Son of God and Son of Man became 'pliant and shaded into one another' to suit their new function.[22]

Despite the somewhat blurred distinction between messiahship and divinity in reference to Jesus, the NT does sometimes nuance one over the other as in the use of Psalm 45 in Heb 1:8-9. The highly christological first chapter of Hebrews has messianic overtones in its reference to anointing, but the primary purpose of the quotations from the Psalms is to articulate the divinity of Christ. There is a similar fluidity to the divine conjugal metaphor; it may include messianic overtones, but the primary deployment of the metaphor

---

[20] Tremper Longman III, 'The Messiah: Explorations in the Law and Writings' in *The Messiah in the Old and New Testaments* (ed. Stanley E. Porter; Grand Rapids: Eerdmans, 2007), 13-34.

[21] S.A. Cummins, 'Divine Life and Corporate Christology: God, Messiah Jesus and the Covenant Community in Paul' in *The Messiah in the Old and New Testaments* (ed. Stanly E. Porter; Grand Rapids: Eerdmans, 2007), 190-209; N.T. Wright, *The New Testament and the People of God* (London: SPCK, 1992), 307-320.

[22] Birger Gerhardsson, 'The Christology of Matthew' in *Who Do You Say That I Am? Essays on Christology* (eds. Mark Allan Powell & David R. Bauer; Louisville: Westminster John Knox, 1999), 14-32, esp. 29.

appears to demonstrate the Christian community's reinterpretation of Jewish monotheism. The early church's reflections following Jesus' resurrection and exaltation led them to identify Jesus directly with the one God of Israel.[23] Accordingly, they identified him with the divine eschatological bridegroom.

## Mark 2:18-22

In this pericope (Matt 9:14-17 and Luke 5:33-39 par.) Jesus portrays himself as a bridegroom whose presence indicates a time of great joy and celebration. Mark places the pericope reasonably close to the christological statement at the beginning of his Gospel, within a series of conflict narratives that emphasise Jesus' divine authority: he defeats evil spirits (1:23-25), forgives sins (2:1-12) and subordinates the Sabbath to physical needs (2:23-3:5). Jesus' presence indicates the in-breaking of the eschatological age and the arrival of the time of salvation, his self-identification as bridegroom reflecting the prophetic use of the metaphor for the eschatological restoration of God's people.

It is unlikely that Jesus' followers recognised the full import of this metaphor prior to his death and resurrection. Nevertheless, Mark's placement of the pericope, amongst other examples of Jesus' activities that were hitherto ascribed only to God, is significant. It suggests that very early, this pronouncement was interpreted as an occasion when Jesus placed himself within the divine identity of the eschatological husband of God's people.

## Matthew 22:1-14

The Parable of the Wedding Banquet combines OT wedding imagery with the eschatological banquet motif of Isa 25:6. The parable demonstrates the fluidity of Jesus' use of the marriage metaphor, its Christology nuanced in terms of divine sonship. Here the bridegroom is distinguished from God (the king), and Matthew's placement of the pericope immediately subsequent to the Parable of the Talents confirms that the king's son should be understood as Jesus. However, Christology is not the focus of the parable and the son's identity as bridegroom is incidental to the main focus of the story.

---

[23] Richard Bauckham, *Jesus and the God of Israel: God Crucified and Other Studies on the New Testament's Christology of Divine Identity* (Grand Rapids: Eerdmans, 2008), 19.

This use of the divine conjugal metaphor moves beyond the person of the bridegroom to the occasion of the wedding and addresses participation in the eschatological promises of God. Those who have been invited to the wedding banquet but presume upon the privilege by failing to respond appropriately are excluded, and the general riff-raff are invited to take their place. We hear echoes of the prophets' indictment of Israel in this; prior to the exile, the people trusted in their identity as God's chosen nation yet failed to respond with covenant obedience and faithfulness. Just as the prophetic warnings were directed particularly at Israel's leaders, so this parable targets the religious leadership who trusted in their position and privilege. The rejection of the person not wearing wedding clothes (22:11-14) reiterates the need for an appropriate response to the gospel invitation.

Like the similar Lukan parable (Luke 14:15-24), the indiscriminate nature of the new banquet invitation reflects the indiscriminate nature of Jesus' offer of salvation. The OT metaphor spoke of an eschatological restoration of the relationship between God and his covenant community, but the NT develops the metaphor by redefining that community in two ways. On the one hand, it restricts participation in the eschatological wedding to those who respond appropriately to the invitation of salvation; on the other, it opens up participation to those who had not expected an invitation. The incorporation of judgement into the promised relationship between God and his people is a significant development of the OT metaphor.

## *Matthew 25:1-13*

The Parable of the Ten Virgins combines the two aspects of divine conjugal imagery already encountered in Matthew: the bridegroom (9:14-15) and the eschatological wedding (22:1-14). Once again, the OT metaphor is refined: membership of the covenant community by birth will not automatically ensure enjoyment of the blessings of the kingdom of heaven. Rather, one's preparedness in terms of repentance and bearing fruit will be the decisive factors, the wise and foolish virgins representing contrasting responses to Jesus prior to his *parousia*.

The analogy of a wedding feast for the kingdom of heaven is a fitting one; wedding feasts were joyous occasions of great celebration, and to be excluded would be a source of inconsolable mourning. As in the Parable of the Wedding Banquet, there are indications that the eschatological wedding will be accompanied by eschatological judgement, a motif absent from the OT's presentation of the metaphor.

The ten virgins were friends or attendants of the bride, and it is particularly interesting that both of Matthew's nuptial parables express participation in the eschatological wedding in terms of guests rather than bride. This perhaps reflects prophetic usage of the conjugal metaphor where there is simultaneously both cohesion and separation between the individual and the corporate. For example, both Isaiah and Hosea address the Israelites concerning their mother (Isa 50:1; Hos 2:2), yet Isaiah makes clear that it is the individuals themselves who are responsible for their mother's divorce, and Hosea pleads with the individuals to change their mother's behaviour.

## *John 2:1-11*

John describes the wedding at Cana as the occasion when Jesus performed the first of his miraculous signs revealing his glory (John 2:11). The provision of an exceedingly large quantity of wine has generally been interpreted as a symbolic action representing the abundant wine of the new kingdom and the arrival of the messianic age of fulfilment (Jer 31:12; Joel 3:18; Amos 9:14).[24] However, a few commentators note the possibility that John's presentation of the event may have deeper theological significance.

J. Ramsey Michaels sees a correspondence between Jesus and the bridegroom of this wedding, suggesting that the bridegroom functions as a surrogate for Jesus who should have received the credit for the banquet master's compliment (2:10).[25] Donald Carson observes that John may intend a connection between this pericope and John 3:27-30 where Jesus is identified as the eschatological bridegroom: 'He graciously makes good the deficiencies of the unknown bridegroom of John 2, in anticipation of the perfect way he himself will fill the role of messianic bridegroom.'[26] Carson does

---

[24] George R. Beasley-Murray, *John* (WBC; Waco: Word, 1987), 36; Raymond E. Brown, *The Gospel According to John: Volume 1 I-XII* (AB; London: Geoffrey Chapman, 1966), 105; Gary M. Burge, *John* (NIV Application Commentary; Grand Rapids, Michigan: Zondervan, 2000), 99; Andreas J. Kostenberger, *John* (BECNT; Grand Rapids: Baker Academic, 2004), 99; Colin G. Kruse, *John: An Introduction and Commentary* (TNTC; Nottingham: Inter-Varsity Press, 2003), 96.

[25] J. Ramsey Michaels, *The Gospel of John* (NICNT; Grand Rapids: Eerdmans, 2010), 152.

[26] D.A. Carson, *The Gospel According to John* (PNTC; Leicester: Apollos, 1991), 173.

not specify whether he uses the term 'messianic' strictly as that which is associated with the Messiah or more loosely as synonymous with 'eschatological,' nor does he expand this light of thought. However, he notices an important link between messianism and the eschatological bridegroom here and it is possible that the miraculous provision of abundant wine in this pericope demonstrates a fusion of messianic activity with the divine identity of Jesus.

It was the responsibility of the bridegroom to supply sufficient food and drink for the week of festivities, yet at this wedding, it was not the bridegroom who ultimately fulfilled the obligations attached to the role, but Jesus. Could it be that part of the theological significance of this pericope lies in Jesus taking on the duties of the bridegroom, thereby aligning himself with that role? Is this a christological identification of Jesus' role as bridegroom? If so, then the pericope not only looks forward to the subsequent signs performed by Jesus, but also looks back to the christological declaration of the gospel's Prologue (1:1-18).

Several factors suggest the plausibility of this hypothesis. The first chapter of John's Gospel makes a number of christological claims: the Prologue describes Jesus as the pre-existent God-incarnate (1:1-2, 14); John the Baptist and Nathanael testify that Jesus is the Son of God (1:34, 49), Peter identifies him as the Messiah (1:41) and Jesus refers to himself using the somewhat ambiguous title 'the Son of Man' (1:51). The full articulation of the title 'Son of Man' and its interface with Jesus' other christological designations required all of Jesus' ministry, life, death, resurrection and exaltation, and John's Gospel concerns itself with precisely this articulation. Accordingly, it is fitting that from the high Christology of the Prologue and introductory narratives, John moves straight into an account of the first miraculous deed which demonstrates Jesus' identity as the divine eschatological bridegroom.

Furthermore, δόξα 'glory' (1:14) provides a verbal connection between the Prologue and the summary of the wedding narrative (2:11). Rudolf Schnackenburg comments that it would be wrong to restrict the glory of Jesus at Cana to the revelation of his divine and miraculous power.[27] He sees a christological emphasis to John's narrative here in which 'the believer experiences something of the

---

[27] Rudolf Schnackenburg, *The Gospel According to St John (1-4)* (New York: Seabury, 1980), 366.

divine being of Jesus, [and] contemplates the majesty of the Son of God.' Whilst Schnackenburg does not link this with Jesus' identity as the divine eschatological bridegroom, it is certainly possible that this verbal correspondence signifies John's intention for the reader to do so.

### John 3:27-29

John the Baptist likened his relationship with Jesus to that between bridegroom's friend and bridegroom. George R. Beasley-Murray and Gary M. Burge deny the Baptist any intentional reference to the OT divine conjugal metaphor.[28] However, it is probable that he is obliquely signalling to his disciples that in Jesus God is betrothing his people to himself in fulfilment of the OT prophecies.[29] Certainly by the time the Gospel was written, it is unlikely that John's readership would have interpreted the Baptist's statements any other way and the cumulative effects of John 1 to 3 indicate that the person of Jesus constituted not only the arrival of the messianic age of fulfillment, but also the arrival of the presence of God.

In summary, conjugal imagery in the gospels builds upon OT usage of the metaphor. All four evangelists use the metaphor christologically, placing Jesus within the identity of the eschatological bridegroom. Matthew's conjugal parables develop the metaphor of the eschatological wedding and redefine participation in terms of individual response to the gospel. They also introduce an element of judgement into an OT metaphor that previously expressed only comfort and hope. The gospels' use of the metaphor focuses on the bridegroom, the wedding, and the guests. Bridal imagery is largely absent and completely undeveloped; we must turn to the Pauline corpus for articulation of this aspect of the metaphor.

## The Pauline Corpus

There are perhaps fewer instances of conjugal imagery within the Pauline corpus than is sometimes assumed. A number of scholars understand Paul's marriage analogy at Rom 7:1-6 as an example of the divine conjugal metaphor.[30] However, the thrust of the analogy

---

[28] Beasley-Murray, *John*, 52; Burge, *John*, 122.

[29] Carson, *The Gospel*, 211; Kruse, *John*, 122; Leon Morris, *The Gospel according to John* (NICNT; Grand Rapids: Eerdmans, 1971), 241.

[30] E.g. James D.G. Dunn, *Romans* (WBC; Waco: Word, 1988), 362; Joseph A. Fitzmyer, *Romans: A New Translation with Introduction and Commentary* (ABD; New York: Doubleday,

is to emphasise the believers' freedom from the law rather than to expound any essentially nuptial nature to their relationship with Christ, and attempts to allegorise Paul's illustration in terms of marriage to Christ are overstated.[31]

Likewise, when Paul argues against sexual immorality (1 Cor 6:12-17) it is not clear that he intends union with Christ to be understood nuptially. Paul's point may simply be that the physical union of a believer with a prostitute is unthinkable because, by the Spirit, the believer's body has become one of Christ's 'limbs' and is to be used for Christ, rather than profaned by illicit sex.[32] This section, therefore, will focus on the two unmistakable examples of divine conjugal imagery within the Pauline corpus: 2 Cor 11:1-3 and Eph 5:25-32.

## 2 Corinthians 11:1-3

In language reminiscent of the OT divine conjugal metaphor, Paul appeals to the exclusive nature of marriage to warn the Corinthians of the threat posed by false teachers. Paul feels a 'godly jealousy' for the Corinthians (2 Cor 11:2). The OT metaphor used a husband's righteous jealousy for his wife to express God's intolerant demand for his people's exclusive devotion to him. Here Paul extends the metaphor to portray himself as the father of the bride, equally concerned to preserve her purity throughout the lengthy betrothal period. His desire to present the church as a chaste virgin to Christ corresponds to the obligation of a Jewish father to protect his daughter's virginity.

This is the first explicit NT reference to the church in marital terms and it coheres with an inaugurated eschatology. Jewish couples were considered legally 'married' during the betrothal period, thus the church currently belongs to Christ alone, but awaits the final consummation of the relationship at the *parousia*. The juxtaposition of the plural ὑμᾶς 'you' with the singular ἑνὶ ἀνδρί 'one husband' emphasises the corporate nature of the betrothal of the Corinthian

---

1992), 459; Robert Jewett *Romans: A Commentary* (Hermeneia, Minneapolis: Fortress, 2007), 434; Thomas R. Schreiner, *Romans* (BECNT, Grand Rapids: Baker Academic, 1998), 345; Tait, *Jesus, the Divine Bridegroom*, 237.

[31] Richard A. Batey, *New Testament Nuptial Imagery* (Leiden: Brill, 1971), 18; Grant R. Osborne, *Romans* (IVP New Testament Commentary; Downers Grove: IVP, 2004), 168.

[32] Gordon D. Fee, *The First Epistle to the Corinthians* (NICNT; Grand Rapids: Eerdmans, 1987), 260; David E. Garland, *1 Corinthians* (BECNT; Grand Rapids: Baker Academic), 233; Leon Morris, *1 Corinthians* (TNTC; rev. ed.; Leicester: IVP), 100.

church to Christ.[33] 'One husband' also highlights the purpose of Paul's marriage metaphor here. He does not employ the imagery to portray the conjugal nature of the Corinthian church's relationship with Christ. Rather, in a similar manner to the prophetic metaphor, the exclusive nature of marriage/betrothal exposes the false teachers, with their different Jesus, different spirit and different gospel (2 Cor 11:4), as illicit lovers who are seducing the church away from her true husband.

### *Ephesians 5:25-32*

This is the passage *par excellence* that describes the relationship between Christ and his church in marital terms. However, the description of Christ and the church in marital union requires some nuancing.

Paul evokes the divine conjugal metaphor of the OT in his command for husbands to love their wives as Christ loved the church (Eph 5:25a).[34] Implicit in this is the command to love unconditionally, recalling God's promise to restore his people under a new covenant even though their spiritual infidelity rendered them unlovely in the extreme.

Paul then shifts his focus from marriage to Christology (5:25b-27). The imagery of washing with water suggests the ceremonial bath that a bride took as part of her wedding preparations, but also corresponds with the cleansing effected by God for Israel in Ezek 16:9-14. The similarities between Ezek 16:9-14 and Eph 5:26-27 are striking: God bathed Israel with water and washed the blood from her, Israel became very beautiful and the splendor God had given her made her beauty perfect.

God's grace was such that he chose to call Israel into covenant relationship with him despite her unpromising beginnings (Ezek 16:1-5). However, the prophet's description of what God had done for Israel emphasised the extent of her debauchery as she spurned God's saving love. Paul, by contrast, now turns Ezekiel's metaphor on its head, the apostle's description of what Christ does for the

---

[33] Murray J. Harris, *The Second Epistle to the Corinthians: A Commentary on the Greek Text* (NICNT; Grand Rapids: Eerdmans, 2005), 737.

[34] Authorship of the Letter to the Ephesians is debated. This paper will refer to the author of Ephesians as Paul, whilst acknowledging that Pauline authorship of this letter is not universally accepted.

church emphasising the extent of her transformation through Christ's saving love.³⁵

The aorist participle καθαρίσας 'cleansing' is a participle of means, clarifying how the church is sanctified (5:26).³⁶ Sanctification for Paul is both a completed action, achieved through the Christ-event (Rom 15:16; 1 Cor 1:2), and an ongoing process which will only be completed at the *parousia* (Rom 6:19; 1 Thess 4:3-8). These 'already' and 'not yet' aspects of sanctification cohere with Paul's use of the divine conjugal metaphor at 2 Cor 11:1-3; the church is betrothed and belongs to Christ, but the final consummation, when she becomes his wife in full, belongs to the eschaton.³⁷

The two ἵνα purpose clauses of vv. 26 and 27 suggest a sequential progression. Some scholars take them as co-ordinate to indicate that Christ's presentation of his bride is effective in the present.³⁸ However, all other biblical instances of two successive ἵνα clauses, which indicate concurrent actions dependent on a common finite verb, use a conjunction such as καί, ἤ or ἀλλά. Thus ἵνα παραστήσῃ 'so that he might present' must be subordinate to the previous purpose clause (ἵνα αὐτὴν ἁγιάσῃ 'in order to sanctify her') and indicates future fulfilment.³⁹ This is consistent with Paul's description of the believers' future presentation to Christ in Col 1:22, 28.

In an abrupt turn, Paul appears to leave behind his betrothed/bride metaphor and speak of the church as already united to Christ as his wife in a one-flesh relationship (Eph 5:31-32). This is difficult to harmonise with the future aspect of v. 27. However, Paul's argument is not that Christ and the church are already in a marriage relationship, but that the one-body relationship between Christ and the church is paradigmatic for the human marriage one-flesh relationship.

---

³⁵ Frank Thielman, *Ephesians* (BECNT; Grand Rapids: Baker Academic, 2010), 386.

³⁶ Clinton E. Arnold, *Ephesians* (ZECNT; Grand Rapids: Zondervan, 2010), 387, Peter T. O'Brien, *Ephesians* (PNTC; Grand Rapids: Eerdmans, 1999), 422.

³⁷ Arnold, *Ephesians*, 389.

³⁸ Earnest Best, *Ephesians: A Shorter Commentary* (Edinburgh: T&T Clark, 2003), 289; Rudolf Schnackenburg, *The Epistle to the Ephesians: A Commentary* (Edinburgh: T&T Clark, 1991), 251.

³⁹ Arnold, *Ephesians*, 389; Markus Barth, *Ephesians 4: A New Translation with Introduction and Commentary* (AB; New York: Doubleday, 1974), 628; O'Brien, *Ephesians*, 424.

In v. 28, Paul exhorts husbands to love their wives because they are one body. The marriage union has rendered them a single unity; therefore, the husband should care for the wife as he would his own body. This causes a shift in Paul's thinking from the church as the bride of Christ back to the church as the body of Christ, an image which Paul had already invoked in his command for wives to submit to their husbands (5:23). Paul now personalises the passage by referring to individuals as members of Christ's body and switching from the third to first person (5:29-30). This appears to be an appeal to Paul's readers to consider the veracity of his argument by recalling the way in which they belong to Christ and how he constantly provides and cares for them, the church, the members of his body.[40]

Paul quotes Gen 2:24 in connection with the church being Christ's body, altering the LXX's ἕνεκεν τούτου 'on account of this' to the synonymous ἀντὶ τούτου to indicate that he uses the quotation in connection with his preceding argument.[41] The logic is that the relationship between Christ and his people as one body is reflected in the permanence and unity of a husband and wife's 'one-flesh' relationship.[42]

This passage interweaves two metaphors for the new covenant community, the bride of Christ (Eph 5:25-27) and the body of Christ (5:28-32). It is significant that individual believers belong to Christ only as members of his body. Paul has previously used bridal imagery of the church, but when he places the individual within his corporate metaphor, he avoids intimating that individuals are to view their own relationship with Christ as marital in nature. This is similar to the way in which the OT maintained a separation between individuals and corporate Israel within the divine conjugal metaphor.

This passage does not demonstrate that the church's current relationship with Christ is that of wife and husband. Rather, it shows that the one-flesh relationship of human marriage, which is characterised by intimacy, permanence and exclusivity, expresses the permanent unity and intimacy that exists between Christ and the church as his body. In fact, Paul implies that the human

---

[40] Arnold, *Ephesians*, 392.

[41] Thielman, *Ephesians*, 389.

[42] Batey, *New Testament*, 31.

marriage relationship was instituted to prefigure the one-body relationship between Christ and the church (5:32).

Like the gospels, the Pauline corpus both adopts and adapts marriage imagery. The prophetic emphasis on the exclusive nature of marriage is prominent in 2 Corinthians. In Ephesians, divine conjugal imagery that previously served to indict is now used for paraenetic purposes. The metaphor is interwoven with the metaphor of the church as the body of Christ and anticipates the future fulfilment of their relationship when Christ will present the church to himself as a radiant bride. Of course, the most developed presentation of the metaphor's future aspect is found in the Revelation of John, to which we now turn.

*Revelation*

Divine conjugal imagery in Revelation 19 and 21 draws heavily upon both OT and NT usage of the metaphor, and the passages are densely packed with allusions and theological significance.

After the conclusion of John's vision concerning the judgement and destruction of Babylon, Rev 19:6-10 introduces a new section on Jesus' return. The mood is joyous, for the long-awaited wedding of the Lamb has come (19:7). The divine conjugal metaphor combines a number of elements already encountered: God's promise to restore his relationship with his covenant people as a new marriage (Isa 54:5-8; 62:5; Ezek 16:60; Hos 2:16-20), the redefinition of the covenant community (Matt 22:1-14; 25:1-13), the eschatological (wedding) feast (Isa 25:6; Matt 22:1-14; Luke 14:15-24), wedding clothes and jewellery (Ezek 16:10-13), and the identification of Jesus as the eschatological bridegroom (Mark 2:19-20 par.; Matt 25:1-13; John 2:1-11; 3:29).

The church is portrayed as the bride of Christ who has prepared herself for her wedding. Her preparations reflect the focus on perseverance and faithfulness in Revelation (19:7) and recall the emphasis of the Matthean parables on the appropriate response to salvation in Christ (Matt 22:1-14; 25:1-13). However, consonant with garments of salvation and righteousness being a gift from God (Isa 61:10), the bride's preparations are not self-driven, but dependent upon the provision of fine linen to wear (Rev 19:8).

The bright, pure linen is the righteous acts of the saints. This is most likely a plenary genitive encompassing both subjective (that performed by the saints) and objective senses (that performed by

God for the saints).[43] Hence the twofold nature of the bride's preparations and the saints' righteous acts reflects the complementary facets of salvation: it is God's work of grace, but believers work out their salvation in fear and trembling as a response (Phil 2:2). The saints' righteous acts are only possible because of their indwelling by the Holy Spirit, thereby reflecting God's promise to contribute righteousness, justice, love, mercy and faithfulness to his relationship with his covenant people (Hos 2:19-20). God's provision of fine clothing here recalls his similar provision for Israel (Ezek 16:10-13) and her ungrateful response. It is a reminder that God's incomprehensible grace and forgiveness in restoring his covenant people lies behind the wedding metaphor. It also recalls Paul's use of the metaphor to demonstrate how the church's presentation as a radiant bride is dependent on Christ's self-giving love (Eph 5:25-27).

The metaphor changes from corporate bride of the Lamb to those individuals invited to the wedding feast (Rev 19:9). Divine conjugal imagery has so far tended to distinguish between the corporate and the individual, and has resisted placing the individual directly within the metaphor of bride. In this respect, John's use of the metaphor is consistent with earlier instances. However, the statement that the bride's fine linen comprises the righteous acts of the saints hints at the placing of individuals within the bridal metaphor, and suggests an approaching alignment of the individual with the corporate in the metaphor of church's marriage to the Lamb.

This is precisely what we see in the final instances of the metaphor in John's vision of the renewal of creation (Revelation 21 and 22). The New Jerusalem is prepared as a bride adorned for her husband (21:2), recalling the imagery of Isa 54, 61 and 62, and Rev 19:6-8. However, immediately following the vision of the corporate bride, God's closeness with his individual people is emphasised (19:3-4).

The New Jerusalem is a city prepared as a bride in 21:3, but a people (the church), the bride/wife of the Lamb in 21:9. Thus the New Jerusalem is best understood as both the redeemed community and their dwelling place.[44] Her re-creation is developed in covenant terms: the people will be God's people and he will be their God

---

[43] G. K. Beale, *The Book of Revelation* (NIGTC; Grand Rapids: Eerdmans, 1999), 936; Grant R. Osborne, *Revelation* (BECNT; Grand Rapids: Eerdmans, 2002), 675.

[44] Osborne, *Revelation*, 733.

(19:3). This is a striking echo of God's promise of restoration in similar terms (Hos 1:10) and recalls the appalling debauchery of Israel's spiritual adultery which caused him to be their God no longer (Hos 1:9). Behind John's vision of the New Jerusalem descending from heaven as a bride lies God's incomprehensible and unprecedented grace and forgiveness.

In the Sinaitic Covenant, God had promised that he would make his dwelling-place among his people (Lev 26:11-12). This was fulfilled in the in-dwelling of believers by the Holy Spirit, but the final consummation of the new covenant comes only in the final age, when what is at present a spiritual reality becomes a physical reality. At last, the bride of the Lamb becomes his wife (Rev 19:9). The physical reality of God dwelling with his people and the tender intimacy with which he treats them (19:3-4) is the result of this final fulfilment of the OT promises. Only in this future reality, at Christ's return, will individuals fully experience intimate communion with God. Significantly, this is the only instance when the promises of the marriage metaphor are directed towards individual believers who are identified with the bridal metaphor.

The Revelation of John completes the biblical marriage metaphor. For the first time, it brings individuals explicitly within the sphere of the metaphor to describe the future intimate communion with God that awaits believers at the return of Christ. Numerous allusions to the marriage metaphor in Isaiah, Hosea and Ezekiel recall not only God's promises of restoration, but also the extent of Israel's spiritual adultery. The OT background to the divine conjugal metaphor demonstrates that the glorious wedding of the bride and the Lamb is the ultimate fulfilment of God's grace and forgiveness.

## Conclusion

Renita Weems observes that the most enduring metaphors are those that tap into widely held, deeply felt values or attitudes within an audience.[45] Hence a metaphor about marriage tends to have lasting value because of the extent to which people are emotionally and socially invested in their intimate relationships with each other.

For an ancient Israelite audience, the power of the metaphor was reinforced by the similar covenantal nature of marriage and Israel's relationship with God. The conceptual premise of the biblical

---

[45] Weems, *Battered Love*, 24.

prophets was that marriage constituted an exclusive covenant relationship, violation of which threatened the stability of Israelite society. By shattering the integrity of the household unit, adultery threatened the vehicle for the bilateral expression of the covenant relationship between God and Israel: literal adultery violated the covenant between Israel and God, just as spiritual adultery did. In a dynamic interplay between the literal and figurative, the prophets produced a unique portrayal of the way in which Israel's heinous sin struck at the foundation of Israel's society. The presentation of Israel's sin in such graphic terms accorded the marriage metaphor an important part in the theodicy developed by prophets such as Jeremiah and Ezekiel. However, the extent of Israel's covenant violation also served to demonstrate the extent of God's grace behind his promised eschatological restoration, which in turn demonstrated his commitment to his relationship with Israel.

The divine conjugal metaphor in the NT incorporates Jesus within the identity of the eschatological bridegroom. The metaphor serves an important christological purpose but the Matthean parables introduce an element of judgement into Israel's restoration such that ethnic identity is neither guarantee nor prohibition of covenant community membership. The Gospels and the Pauline corpus avoid personalizing the marriage metaphor; only in Revelation is the individual placed within the divine conjugal metaphor.

The OT background to divine conjugal imagery is critical to understanding the NT metaphor. It is evident in Paul's appeal to his divine jealousy for the Corinthians' purity and is strikingly inverted to show the Ephesians the extent of Christ's saving action on behalf of his church. Understanding the conjugal metaphor in light of the prohibition against taking back a wife who had remarried (Deut 24:1-4) lends richness to marriage language in Revelation which is, in addition, heavily laced with Isaianic allusions. Rather than illustrating an essentially nuptial relationship between God and his covenant community, the divine conjugal metaphor takes up the theme of grace that pervades the story of salvation history and primarily demonstrates the incalculable forgiveness shown by the God of second chances to a sinful people.

## Invitation for Papers

This inaugural issue of MST's journal *PARADOSIS* brings together theological minds in the on-going advancement in Christian thought and practice. We believe that theological and biblical disciplines should never exist on their own; they require a broader field of vision. Therefore *PARADOSIS* will showcase articles in Biblical studies and Theology which manifest this.

Particular interest will be shown in those submissions which are of an inter-disciplinary nature especially those that connect Biblical, historical or theological insights with current church trends or challenges to Christian thought in a wide variety of current contexts.

The majority of papers in each edition will coalesce around certain themes and the Executive Editor will receive suggestions regarding potential future themes or guest authors for individual issues. Each issue will have its own Issue Editor on her/his own field of expertise (proposed themes for the coming years are listed below). In this way the journal will examine reasonable expressions of the proposed theme from the range of theological disciplines, framework and perspective to suit a scholarly, student or pastoral readership.

Articles accepted for publication are 'peer reviewed', being read and assessed by at least one pertinent scholar in the appropriate field.

We extend our invitation to all, both in Australia and internationally.

Dr Justin Tan

Executive Editor

2015: *Studies in the Psalms*

2016: *Christology*

2017: *Christian/Biblical Ethics*

# Notes for Contributors

**Submission requirements:**

Manuscript

    Papers should not exceed 8000 words, although the Editor retains the discretion to publish papers that vary from this length.

    It is preferable that submissions be prepared in Microsoft Word format.

All papers are to be written in English, and must conform to MST style requirements. This can be found on the MST website (http://www.mst.edu.au/content/style-guide-paradosis-mst-press). Refer also to the style used in the current issue.

    Greek and Hebrew words must be written in original script using *SBL Greek/Hebrew* Unicode font. An English translation should be provided in brackets where the meaning is not readily apparent from the context. No transliteration is to be provided.

    Authors are advised to use gender inclusive and non-discriminatory language.

    Any visuals should be integrated into the document, or sent separately as separate jpg or gif files with an explanation as to their position in the paper.

Submission

    Papers to be considered for inclusion are to be submitted directly to the Executive Editor (jtan@mst.edu.au), via electronic mail.

    A declaration that the submitted articles are your own work and that you have acknowledged the work/s of others used in the articles in the references, etc. must be included with any submission.

    A covering letter that includes the author's full name, titles, affiliations, with complete mailing addresses, including email, telephone and facsimile numbers, should be attached to the paper.

Review of Submissions

All submissions will be sent to referees for anonymous recommendation.

The Editor holds the right to make editorial corrections to accepted submissions.

## Copyright

*PARADOSIS* is published by MST Press, the publishing arm of the Melbourne School of Theology. The copyright for any published papers will remain with the author. MST publishes these papers on the following conditions:

- They do not appear elsewhere (including web pages) for 12 months from the date of publication in *PARADOSIS*.
- Whenever they are printed elsewhere (including web pages), the following notice will be included: "This article first appeared in the __ issue of the *PARADOSIS* series".
- MST retains the right to use the paper in any MST publications, reprints, or in electronic form (ie. Online, CD-Rom, etc.).
- MST retains the right to use a portion or description of the paper with the author's name in our promotional material.
- Authors are themselves responsible for obtaining permission to reproduce copyright material from other sources.
- The author will be presented with one copy of the publication.

## Disclaimer

The opinions and conclusions published in the *PARADOSIS* series are those of the authors and do not necessarily represent the views of the Editors or the Melbourne School of Theology.